The Navigator's Art

A. B. A. HUTSON

Illustrated by Alec Davis

 Mills & Boon Ltd London

First published in Great Britain 1974 by
Mills & Boon Limited, 17–19 Foley
Street, London W1A 1DR

© A. B. A. Hutson 1974

ISBN 0 263 05592 2

Printed in Great Britain by
Clarke, Doble & Brendon Ltd,
Plymouth

Contents

Page

1 **How it all started**   5
   The Mediterranean, the cradle of navigation

2 **The northern sailors**   14
   The Scandinavians and the Irish monks

3 **The great canoe navigators of the Pacific**   23
   Polynesian navigation

4 **Not by guesswork alone**   31
   The compass and the chart

5 **Indies East and Indies West**   41
   Christopher Columbus; early navigational aids

6 **All the way round**   58
   Magellan, Drake and others

7 **Time is longitude and longitude is time**   69
   The major problem is solved

8 **From Cook to Sumner**   85
   The art is improved

9 **Navigation today**   98
   Electrical aids to navigation

10 **Through the air**   114
   The problems of navigating an aeroplane, and how they
   have been solved

11 **Mind the rocks!**   131
   The art of pilotage; how to fix the ship's position;
   lighthouses, buoys, tides; some errors lead to disaster

12 How do animals and birds navigate?   173
     Swallows, pigeons, eels and bees; Pioneer 10—messages
     to outer space

Appendix A   Making a quadrant   181

Appendix B   Making an astrolabe   182

Appendix C   Making a sextant   185

Appendix D   Stars in the northern sky   189

Appendix E   Latitude and longitude   190

A short bibliography   191

Index   192

CHAPTER 1

How it all started

No-one can be sure when navigation first began. The earliest mention of the seaman's skill comes from the Greek historian Herodotus. He told how men let down a weighted line with a lump of tallow on the tip of the weight. The length of the line paid out gave the depth of water, and the yellow mud sticking to the tallow told the pilot that they were approaching the Nile.

An Egyptian craft with a sounding rod.

Odysseus navigated by the stars.

Egyptians sailed the waters of the Nile for many years before Herodotus wrote of the lead and line. In tomb paintings their high-ended craft sail in procession up and down the river. At the bow stand two men, one feeling out the depth of water with a long, slim pole while the other directs the helmsman by means of hand signals. When sailing the Red Sea, the pole could be used to push the bow away from the treacherous coral heads that speared up so suddenly.

Odysseus, the hero of Homer's epic poem, was the first sailor to steer by the stars. When he left Calypso's Isle, in the far west near the Straits of Gibraltar, he

'. . . spread his sail to catch the wind and used his seamanship to keep the boat straight with the steering oar. There he sat and never closed his eyes in sleep, but kept them on the Pleiades or watched the late setting Arcturus and the Great Bear . . . So for seventeen days he sailed upon his course.'

These ancient sailors made rough calculations of the altitude of stars, and, to give another observer bearings of a distant object, used different parts of the hand held out at arm's length. The middle finger of a man's hand would cover 2° whilst his fist represented 8°.

By the fourth century B.C. men had begun to write down directions for sailing from place to place in the Mediterranean. King Darius of Persia planned to attack Greece and sent out a survey party to describe the Greek coastline. The Persians were not a sea-going people and therefore Darius chose Phoenicians for the task. The Greek and Phoenician traders pooled their knowledge of Mediterranean navigation and compiled the 'Periplous'; much later, at the beginning of the third century A.D., an even more detailed book of sailing instructions called the 'Stadiasmus of the Great Sea' was written. The ships in those days sailed from headland to headland, very rarely out of sight of land:

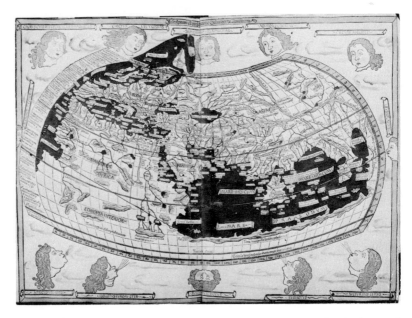

Ptolemy's world map, first drawn in the second century A.D., had to wait 1,300 years before publication. The *Geographical Magazine,* October 1971.

'... coasting from the Pillars of Hercules to Cape Hermea is two days ... From Zygris to Ladamantia 20 stadia [2 miles approx]; close by lies a rather large island: put in with this on your right. There is a harbour accessible with any wind: water is to be found.'

When the voyage lay offshore, across the Great Sea, the ship waited for a favourable wind. In the early days there

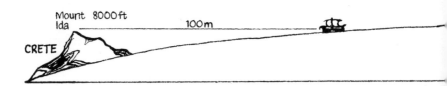

were no such directions as N., S., E., W., and winds were named after the places from which these winds blew. So the wind that blew from Africa to Europe was called 'Africus'. Now, of course, we simply name the wind from the direction from which it comes; so a NW wind blows *from* the North West.

Ships' sails were clumsy, billowing squares suitable only when the wind was astern; they were difficult to handle and dangerous in strong winds. In heavy weather the yard was lowered and the men took to the oars. Once they had made their 'crossing', out of sight of land, the pilot had to recognise landmarks and then direct his course to the port. Beacons were lit on hill tops when ships were expected, whilst at the great port of Alexandria at the mouth of the Nile a 500-foot tower, the Pharos, guided ships by night and day towards the low-lying shore that had no natural landmarks.

Built about 280 B.C., the Pharos stood until destroyed by an earthquake in the fourteenth century A.D. The clear sunny weather of the Mediterranean summer made the pilot's task easier when sailing towards Greece from Egypt, for the peak of Mount Ida, in Crete, 8,000 feet high, was visible for 100 miles. Once close to shore, local fishermen would give more precise directions, but woe to the pilot that put his ship in danger; the sailors had the right to execute him without further ado.

Perhaps the greatest voyage of these ancient navigators was the first complete circumnavigation of Africa, as commanded by Prince Necos, between 610 and 595 B.C. Sailing and rowing and keeping close to shore, the

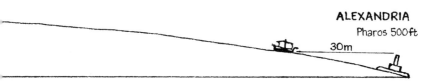

Though Egypt and Crete are more than 300 miles apart, seamen sailed only one or two days out of sight of land.

Phoenicians made their slow way around the coast. At one point they stopped, planted crops and harvested them for stores to continue their voyage. When they returned their adventures were recorded by Herodotus:

> 'On their return the sailors reported (others may believe them but I will not) that in sailing from East to West around Africa they had the Sun on their *right* hand.'

This simple idea was not easily accepted. However, these early navigators had undoubtedly ventured south of the Tropic of Capricorn and seen the sun shining in the northern sky.

An even more remarkable achievement of this same Prince Necos was the digging of the first Suez Canal, which was finally finished by the Persian conqueror, Darius. The canal was so wide that two triremes could be rowed abreast. Before it was completed, though, Necos was warned by a prophet that his work would only benefit a barbarian invader. By that time 120,000 Egyptians had died at the diggings. Thousands of years later, in 1866, another 120,000

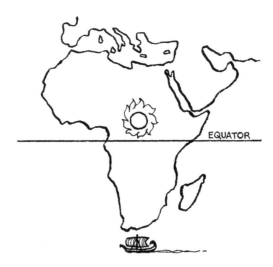

Never before had the sun been seen in the northern sky; but no one believed the story.

An Irish curragh and a Welsh coracle.

died digging the present canal under the Frenchman De Lesseps, and during the excavations there was discovered a carved stone—the Stele of Darius. On it was recorded the opening of that first canal:

'Saith King Darius: "I am a Persian. From Persia I conquered Egypt. I ordered this canal to be dug from the river called the Nile which flows in Egypt to the sea which goes from Persia. So this canal was dug, as I commanded, and ships went from Egypt to Persia, according to my desire." '

Though the Mediterranean has been called the 'cradle of navigation', the Phoenicians were very soon venturing beyond the Straits of Gibraltar, and by 600 B.C. were regularly trading with the Cornish tin miners. There they saw men who sailed to the 'Holy Isle' (Ireland) in skin boats. Today, coracles of canvas stretched over a willow frame are still used in parts of Wales, and in the Aran Isles and the West of Ireland larger curraghs are used because they can so easily be carried ashore out of reach of the wild Atlantic gales.

A Greek, Pytheas of Massilia, even voyaged as far north as Iceland, telling how the 'barbarians showed us where the sun goes to rest . . . in those regions the night was quite short, consisting in some places of two hours, in others of three . . . ' He saw the fog-covered edges of the sea-ice and its continual grating roar suggested to his ears the breathing of some terrifying undersea monster.

During all their voyages, men could observe evidence that the earth was a globe. Mathematicians and astronomers

A   B   FLAT EARTH VIEW

SHIP MUST SAIL TO A₁ BEFORE SHE IS VISIBLE   CURVED
                                                    EARTH VIEW

Is the earth flat or round?

12

had known this for many years, but few ordinary men believed it. Even landsmen must have noticed that the ship with the tallest mast was seen first, which, if the earth was flat, would make no difference. Sailors noticed that as they sailed southwards the stars revolving around the pole became lower and lower, but, if they sailed north more and more seemed to circle the pole, whilst the southern stars disappeared from the heavens.

All these practical proofs were to be submerged by the rulings of the Church courts, which supported the 'flat earth' theory in which, even today, some people still believe.

CHAPTER 2

The northern sailors

The seamen who steered their course across the North Atlantic were faced with many more problems than those who sailed the Mediterranean. First, there was no 'sailing season' when good weather could be relied on. Though the wind can blow just as strongly in the Mediterranean, the waves do not have the 'fetch', the distance they need to build up in size; when a storm in the Atlantic begins to blow,

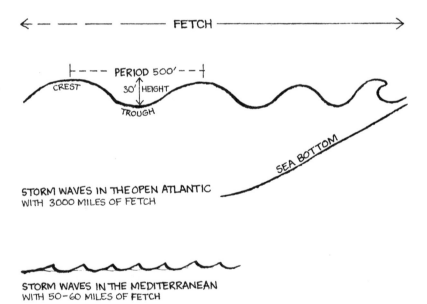

STORM WAVES IN THE OPEN ATLANTIC
WITH 3000 MILES OF FETCH

STORM WAVES IN THE MEDITERRANEAN
WITH 50–60 MILES OF FETCH

Atlantic waves compared with Mediterranean waves.

or a hurricane is brewing in the Caribbean, the waves travel across the Atlantic to dash themselves on the coasts of Europe and Britain, even though the weather there is calm. When accompanied by a storm the waves may reach a height of fifty feet in the open sea.

Secondly, the northern sailors were not able to use the sun or stars with such accuracy as the Mediterranean sailors, as there is a great difference between their summer and

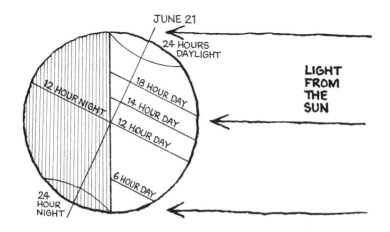

The length of day and night from Equator to poles.

winter risings and settings, both in time and direction. The length of daylight in northern Scotland varies between six hours in the winter to nineteen hours during the summer, whereas there is less than an hour's difference between winter and summer daylight in the Mediterranean. The long daylight hours were of value to some:

'. . . at the Summer Solstice . . . the setting sun hides itself as if behind a little hill, so that no darkness occurs . . . but whatever task a man wishes to perform, even to picking the lice out of his shirt, he can manage it precisely as in broad daylight.'

15

But the biggest problem of all, and the most surprising to the Mediterranean sailors when they sailed north, was the tide, for the Mediterranean is almost tideless. Julius Caesar's ships were safely moored—he thought—but the ebb (outgoing) tide, helped by the wind, left them stranded on the rocks. Not only did the water rise and fall as much as forty feet, but in doing so it formed vast tidal currents like great rivers and when flowing fast across an uneven patch of sea-bed, or against some outflow from a river, terrifying tide-rips would form where the waves heaped themselves and plunged in every direction regardless of wind. Off headlands tidal races, such as Portland Race, are still avoided by the largest ships.

Of all the early navigators St. Brendan was the most trusting. According to legend he set out with a small band of monks to seek the Island of the Paradise of the Saints. They sailed in a small boat of ox-hide and among their stores they took butter to grease the hides to keep them waterproof. For twelve days they sailed NE from Ireland with a following wind, and then rowed when the wind died away. They rowed till exhausted and then set the sail and lay down. A breeze sprang up, though they had no way of telling from what direction. They trusted in 'God, our pilot and steersman'. They visited many islands, one of which was volcanic (perhaps Iceland?). They lit a fire on one small islet only to find it was a very cross whale. They sailed northwards until the sea began to freeze, to be saved by a switch in the wind that blew them southward again. After seven long and weary years St. Brendan found his isle, far to the west, and for centuries to come St. Brendan's Isle appeared on charts; but no-one could ever quite agree where it should be.

Though the Egyptians, Phoenicians and Persians made use of the regular wind pattern in the Red Sea, blowing from the north during the summer and shifting gradually to the south or south-east during the winter months, it was the Vikings and Arabs who made the greatest use of 'homing' winds. The Vikings sailed west from Scandinavia, past

St. Brendan and the whale. Part myth, part legend, part fact.

Scotland, past Ireland, beyond the Faeroes to Iceland, Greenland and even to North America. The Arabs established trading routes to India by making use of the seasonal SW monsoon on their outward journey and returning with the NE monsoon.

The Norsemen soon discovered that by keeping to a northerly course they could be almost sure of a following wind to take them westwards during the summer months. In the autumn they sailed south until they reached the belt of westerly winds which sped them home. Of course their early discoveries were usually the result of an easterly gale that drove them far to the west. Iceland was discovered and settled by Garda, a Danish trader, who whilst sailing to the Faeroes for sheep was driven far beyond his destination. Later, so the sagas say:

'. . . a great Viking named Floki went to search for Garda's Holme [island]. He went first to the Shetlands. Floki took three ravens. The first to be set free flew over the stern and back the way they had come. The second flew up into the air and back to the ship again.'

So they sailed on further to the west; 'but the third bird flew forth straightway over the stem [bow] in the direction

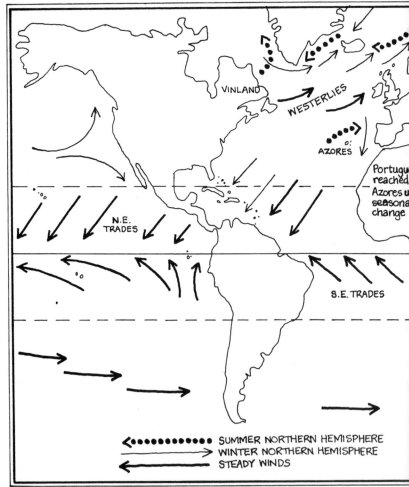

VINLAND

WESTERLIES

AZORES

Portugu[e]
reach[e]d
Azores u[...]
seasona[l]
change

N.E.
TRADES

S.E. TRADES

<•••••••••• SUMMER NORTHERN HEMISPHERE
————————> WINTER NORTHERN HEMISPHERE
<———————— STEADY WINDS

Seasonal winds helped the early navigators, once they had learned that the wind change could be relied on.

where they found the land . . . They called the land Iceland, because in the spring Floki climbed a high mountain and saw a frith [firth—estuary] full of drift ice'.

The name Greenland seems an odd name to give to a country so near to the Arctic Circle, a country almost completely covered with a thick mantle of ice and snow and great glaciers that slide slowly to the sea. Yet once it had a much warmer climate; the west coast areas were green

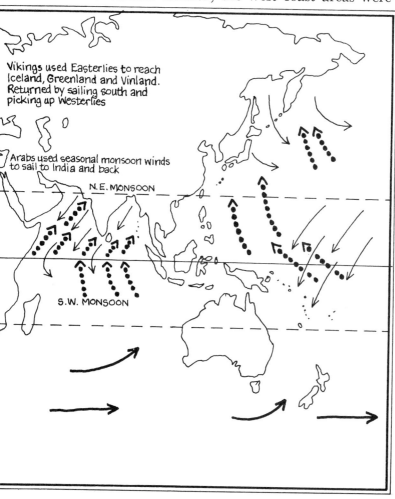

Vikings used Easterlies to reach Iceland, Greenland and Vinland. Returned by sailing south and picking up Westerlies

Arabs used seasonal monsoon winds to sail to India and back

N.E. MONSOON

S.W. MONSOON

with crops growing and pasture land. Eirik the Red, banished first from Norway and then from Iceland for manslaughter, sailed to these west coast inlets and soon small settlements sprang up and ships sailed regularly from Iceland to Greenland during the summer. Again the steadiness of the summer winds from the north-east made this voyage quite simple, for the high volcano, Snaefellsness, on the western tip of Iceland, was visible for two days' sail. One day later they released their birds to show the direction of the land and then the following day the even higher mountains of Greenland were sighted.

Noah and Floki used birds to find land.

When the weather changed, however, no-one quite knew where they would end up. Bjarni, sailing from Norway to join his father in Greenland, heard that his father had already left. He decided to carry on and spend the winter in Greenland at his father's house. Once they had left Iceland behind, '. . . the following wind died down, and north winds and fog overtook them, so that they had no idea which way they were going'. This continued for many days, but eventually they saw the sun and could then get their bearings. They now hoisted sail, and sailed that day before sighting land, and debated among themselves what this land could be. Bjarni decided that this was not Greenland, 'for there are very big glaciers reported to be in Greenland', but this was low-lying land, heavily wooded. Bjarni would not let his men land and a south-west wind sprang up behind them and they sailed away from this new shore for three days. They sighted mountains and glaciers, but still Bjarni was not convinced that he had made his way back to Greenland. Again they sailed out to sea and four days later they came to the cape where Bjarni's father, Herjolf, lived and their voyage of 'discovery' ended.

Bjarni was a farmer and a trader—he was not an explorer. He didn't realise that he had discovered a new 'world'. Leif Eiriksson (Leif, son of Eirik the Red) was eager to explore these new lands to the west and he bought Bjarni's ship. With thirty-five men he set sail, retracing the course of Bjarni's return. They reached the wooded low-lying land and named it Markland ('Woodland'). They sailed further south and discovered a river that flowed from a small lake near the shore. For safety they hauled their ship up into the lake and set about exploring. They found bigger salmon than they had ever seen before and lush pastures where grass grew throughout the winter, for there was no frost. So ideal did it all seem that they decided to spend the winter there, and they set about building a house (Leifsbudir). As autumn came on they continued to explore the new country and one day Tyrkir, the German, came back with the

Following migrating geese.

news that he had found grapes growing there. In the spring Leif and his crew sailed back to Greenland with a cargo of dried grapes (raisins), having named their 'newfoundland' Vinland or Wineland. All the evidence seems to point to the northern tip of Newfoundland as Leif Eiriksson's Vinland.

Though the Vikings made many long voyages and settled in many areas, their voyages were never very far from land, and if the sky was overcast or if they were caught by fogs, then they were truly lost. It has been suggested, though it is difficult to prove, that many of their voyages followed the migration path of the geese and ducks, which wintered in the south and flew north during the summer months to breed. Though their ships could not keep up with the birds, the flocks passing overhead would have enabled the navigators to keep a check on their course.

CHAPTER 3

The great canoe navigators of the Pacific

Of all the early navigators the Polynesians had the most hazardous, most extensive and least protected 'cradle' in which to learn their craft. Luckily it was a 'Pacific' ocean.

Forced out from the mainland of SE Asia by the rapid expansion of population in Northern China, which led to the formation of the great Chinese Empire, groups of

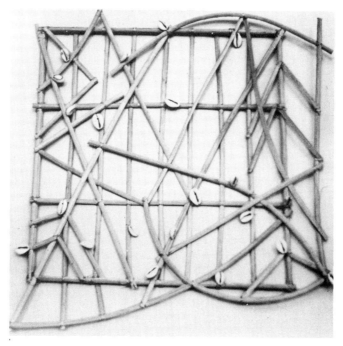

A twig chart from the Marshall Islands.

fugitives had by 1000 B.C. settled in New Guinea, the Philippines, Indonesia and Papua. So far they had been island-hopping. Before them lay the vast expanses of the Pacific. Gradually, they moved east, setting out to find islands beyond the horizon, guided by the flights of birds. Once a large area had been settled, the amazing art of Polynesian navigation began to flourish. It was an art, an art improved by years of experience—it was not a science, for the Polynesians had no written language, i.e. no way of writing down sailing directions for others to follow.

Some had a most ingenious way of making a chart. The natives of the Marshall Islands made charts from twigs, bound together with fibre. Long, straight twigs showed the direction in which islands were to be found and the islands were cowrie shells tied to the framework. Curved strips showed how wave directions were altered by islands, whilst currents were short, straight strips.

Another very simple instrument, found in Hawaii, was known as the 'sacred calabash'. A gourd, a simple bowl, was drilled with a series of holes midway between the bottom and the rim. A slightly larger sighting hole was bored above these and on the rim a small notch was carved. Having filled the bowl to the level of the ring of holes the navigator

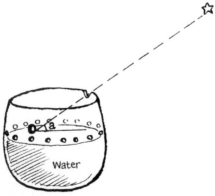

The sacred calabash, forerunner of the bubble sextant (see p. 124). The angle â between the sighting hole and the rim notch was equal to the latitude of Hawaii. The ring of small holes ensured that when filled with water to that level, the calabash was held level.

The inside of a 'navigation school' as it might have appeared on the Gilbert and Ellice Islands.

viewed the Pole Star through the viewing hole. When the Pole Star rested snugly in the notch, then the canoe was in the same latitude as Hawaii. Though this was probably used for short inter-island voyages in the Hawaiian group, no other calabash like this was found anywhere else in

Polynesia, so it is not possible to say if this method was used on longer voyages. The main difficulty was that this calabash could only be used with the Pole Star which could not be seen in the South Pacific, where most of the islands are situated. There is a tiny star close to the South Pole (Sigmar Octans), but it is so small that it can hardly be seen with the naked eye.

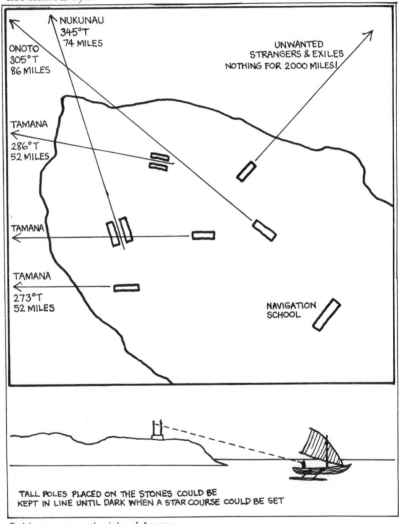

Guide stones on the isle of Arorae.

Can you see three indicators of land?

The Polynesians trained navigators from an early age and they learned long lists of stars by which to steer to other islands. In the Gilbert and Ellice islands the interior of the 'Navigation School' was like a modern planetarium. Every group of stars (constellation) was marked in the thatchwork of the roof and the young navigators had then to learn their positions. Only when they had thoroughly mastered these were they taken to the eastern beach to watch the constellations rise from the ocean as the night progressed.

On the isle of Arorae, in the Gilbert and Ellice group, voyages were always begun from the NW tip where a group of stones had been set up. Each stone showed the bearing (direction) of a nearby island. The canoes set out in the early evening so that before the stones were out of sight the first stars were showing. During the voyage the navigator noted the wind direction, the run of the waves and the shadows of the rigging. Many of the low-lying atolls were difficult to see, but as they were often in groups this made them easier to find. High volcanic islands were much easier to locate. Signs such as land birds were looked for; the green tinge to the base of a cloud would pinpoint a shallow, land-locked lagoon many miles distant, though the atoll was below the horizon, whilst the rich variety of aromas coming from a tropical island could often be savoured a full day's sail away.

Navigation for the Polynesian was not a matter of pin-point accuracy and he rarely set a course for a particular island but rather for a group of islands. However, the Polynesians' canoes were frail and the success of their voyages depended very much on fine weather. Rain, high winds, or just an overcast sky could lead to disaster. As a result the Polynesian developed a great sensitivity to the weather and was able to forecast with some accuracy for up to three days ahead.

When the Polynesians set out on longer voyages they sailed in much larger double canoes known as 'tongiaki' or 'kalia'. Two hulls were strongly lashed together and over them a small platform of planks was laid. On this deck a low rounded shelter was raised, thatched with leaves. Each hull could be as long as 100 feet and so deep that the men who were constantly bailing out had to climb the sides to throw the water out. The triangular sail, very like the lateen sail of the Arabs, was set on a short forked mast and the rigging was fastened to poles that stretched far out over the water on either side. They were very fast, as an early description says:

'The rig of these vessels is so excellent and they go so well under sail that there are few ships in Holland that could overhaul them. They steer them by means of two oars at the stern, one for each canoe.'

Nobody knows how the Polynesians first discovered New Zealand, lying far to the south of their usual tracks and far beyond the normal range of their voyaging. Some of these

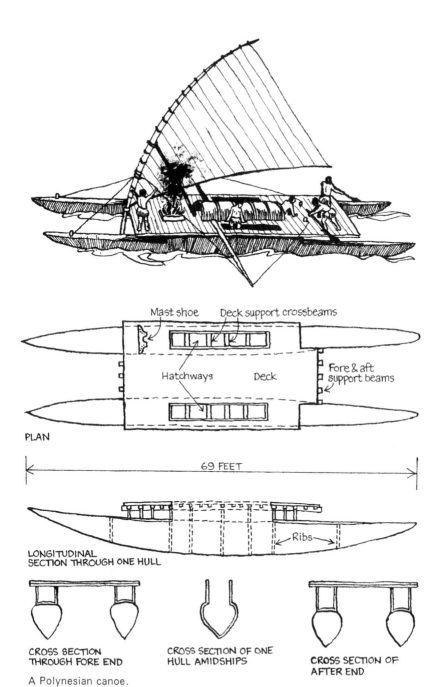

Mast shoe   Deck support crossbeams

Hatchways   Deck

Fore & aft
support beams

PLAN

69 FEET

LONGITUDINAL
SECTION THROUGH ONE HULL

Ribs

CROSS SECTION
THROUGH FORE END

CROSS SECTION OF ONE
HULL AMIDSHIPS

CROSS SECTION OF
AFTER END

A Polynesian canoe.

earliest navigators did, however, manage to return to Polynesia after storms had driven them to the south and west, to the strange new land. Legend tells that the first discoverer of New Zealand, Kupe, told others who wished to reach the new islands to steer to the right of the setting sun on the Orongonui (28th) of Tatua-uruora (November).

Why did the Polynesians attempt such long voyages in such small and seemingly frail craft? Natives from the small island of Mauke in the Cook Islands made a 400-mile return journey for the good fishing, birds' eggs and feathers. Some islands were even stripped of their coconut palms so that stray visitors would not bother to land and so discover the wealth of fish and birds. Because of the soft nature of the coral of which many of the islands consist, stone, especially hard stone that would take a cutting edge, was highly prized for axes and adzes. Long voyages were sometimes made purely for social reasons, but more often it was a war-party seeking vengeance. The natives of the tiny island of Aana terrorised the neighbouring islands to north, east and south to a distance of four hundred miles! Many Polynesians migrated to get away from such neighbours. Once the majority of islands had been settled the need for long voyages lessened, and by the time the Europeans arrived in the Pacific, such voyages and large double canoes were slowly dying out, and the art of long distance navigation gradually faded.

CHAPTER 4

Not by guesswork alone

Remarkable though they were, the voyages of the Polynesian, Viking and early Mediterranean navigators were really calculated guesswork. Science and mathematics were not as important as careful observation, a good memory and luck.

Soon after A.D. 1000 science and mathematics began to influence navigation, although it seemed much more like magic than science:

'When clouds prevent sailors from seeing Sun or star, they take a needle and press its point on the magnet stone. Then they transfix it through a straw and place it in a basin of water. The stone is then moved round and round the basin faster and faster, until the needle, which follows it, is whirling swiftly. At this point the stone is suddenly snatched away, and the needle turns its point towards the Stella Maris. From that position it does not move.'

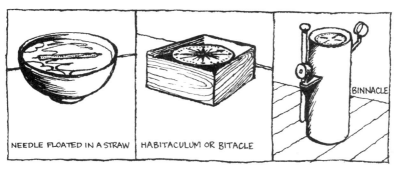

NEEDLE FLOATED IN A STRAW | HABITACULUM OR BITACLE | BINNACLE

The development of the compass.

'Then they transfix it through a straw and place it in a basin of water.'

This account of how sailors made use of a simple magnetic compass was written by the Dominican monk Thomas of Cantimpré about the year 1240. The Stella Maris (Star of the Sea), is of course the Pole Star. Some people of that time believed that it was the Pole Star itself that attracted the needle. Others believed that the inside of the 'lodestone' was like the earth spinning in the firmament, so that it had its own axis and its own poles. Peter Peregrinus, a thirteenth century French soldier and pilgrim, believed that if a magnet could be very accurately cut and mounted by a gem-cutter and set up in line with the axis of the earth then the magnet would revolve at the same speed as the earth and so be a most accurate clock, that would never need winding—an early idea of perpetual motion.

Though Thomas of Cantimpré wrote his description in 1240, sailors had already obtained a magnetic needle balanced on a pivot. Imagine trying to follow the antics of a straw in a bowl of water in a storm! Alexander Neckham, another monk, wrote in 1180:

'They also have a needle placed upon to a dart, and it is turned and whirled round until the point of the needle looks north-east. And so the sailors know which way to steer when Cynosura is hidden by clouds.'

The Chinese 'in dark weather . . . looks at the South-pointing needle'.

By the time these monks were writing, the 'needle' was a standard part of the ship's equipment, housed in its 'habitaculum', soon shortened to 'bitacle', and to this day the compass housing is known as the 'binnacle'. A later improvement was to glue magnetised wires to the underside of a compass card and to pivot the card itself, making the compass steadier and easier to read.

Mathematics influenced navigation in several ways. For centuries the mathematical skill of the Greeks had been lost to Western civilisation because the Church regarded it as one of the 'black arts'. Even Pope Sylvester II was regarded as a magician because he charted the movements of the stars. The Syrians preserved the Greek learning by translating the old mathematical works from Greek into Syrian, and later the Arabs who conquered the Syrians spread the study of mathematics throughout their Empire. They set up observatories and collected all their hard-won knowledge in vast libraries.

The Italians, as well as gathering together mathematical knowledge during this period, collected all the sailing directions for the Mediterranean. Using these, with the newly-discovered skill in mathematics and the use of the compass which would give a reasonably accurate north point, they drew up the first chart. The oldest surviving chart is the Carta Pisana which dates from about A.D. 1275.

Until this time map makers had drawn their maps to fit the shape of the parchment or skin on which they were

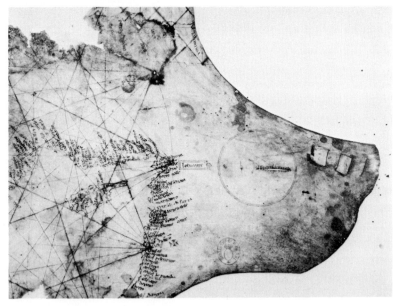

Above: The Carta Pisana. Courtesy of the Bibliothèque Nationale, Paris.
Below: Part of the chart, showing one of the two small scales.

drawing, or to fit within a circle or oval. There was no true scale and important areas or cities were magnified, whilst large areas of little importance shrank. A chart to be of any use had to be accurate, and to show distances it had to be drawn to scale. Chart collections gained the odd name of *waggoners* from a series published by a Dutchman Lucas Janszoon Waghenaer in 1584.

The Carta Pisana, like all other maps and charts of the time, was drawn on sheepskin parchment. The coastline and islands of the Mediterranean were drawn and then an intricate pattern of radiating lines of different colours was laid out over the entire region so that the direction or 'bearing' of one port from another could easily be picked out. The two small circles, one containing a vertical line, the other a horizontal line, were two scales. If the parchment was wetted then it would shrink, and it might not shrink evenly. The actual method of making a chart is described in 'Arte De Navigar', written in 1551 by Martin Cortes for the students of the Seville Nautical Academy.

'... For making Cardes of the Sea ... it shall bee requisite to knowe two things ... the right position of places ... and the distances that is from one place to another.'

First the parchment, sheep or goatskin, was quartered with two heavy black lines at right angles. If the chart were French or Arabian the south would be at the top. Tracing paper was made by rubbing thin paper with linseed oil, and carbon paper by giving a sheet of paper a 'smoky' coating by holding it over burning pitch. With these the coastline was marked out, pricking through the tracing paper with a steel bodkin. The outline was inked in and the parchment cleaned by rubbing it with breadcrumbs. Next came the delicate task of filling in the names of capes, bays, straits, towns and cities with their banners and their coats-of-arms. Lastly, and most important of all, was the drawing of the 'compasses'. The central compass was drawn with its centre where the two heavy black lines crossed. The circumference was drawn in lightly with a piece of lead, forerunner of today's pencil, so that it could be rubbed out later.

Next the rhumbs were drawn in. These represented the winds from NW, NE, SW and SE, and were drawn with green or blue ink. Then came the quarter winds, NNE, ENE, ESE, and so on. Where each of these rhumbs crossed the circumference of the central compass smaller 'compasses' were drawn, each with its own set of rhumb lines. On large charts there would be thirty-two of these small compasses and the chart would be criss-crossed with 512 coloured rhumb lines. Once these lines were inked in the circumference of the centre compass was rubbed out and its cardinal points elaborately decorated. North was usually a fleur-de-lys, east a cross, while west and south were shown by their initial letter only.

A compass rose.

Gerard Mercator (1512–1594). Engraving by Franz Hogenberg, National Maritime Museum.

To use one of these charts the pilot laid his ruler from his point of departure to his destination. He then sought out, using dividers for accuracy, the rhumb line most nearly parallel to his ruler. Once found he traced the line back to the compass rose from which it originated and so read off his course. Modern charts still have compass roses printed in several places, but the rhumb lines are missing, for today's navigator uses parallel rulers, divided and hinged so that they can be moved across the chart and still remain on the same bearing. However, these rulers were not invented until 1584, by a Frenchman called Mordente, and they were not widely used for another hundred years or more.

The more accurate the chart makers tried to make their charts, the more problems and difficulties arose. First, the earth is a sphere and to show the shape of a curved surface on a flat parchment caused some difficulty. Coastlines along the Equator were quite simple but further north or south the distortion of the land masses becomes greater. This is most noticeable on a Mercator projection where Greenland appears to be far greater in area than India, whereas, if you check on a globe, India is in fact larger than Greenland. In spite of this distortion in high latitudes the Mercator projection is the most widely used in navigation. For polar navigation gnomic charts are preferable.

The reason for the distortion in the Mercator projection is quite simple. The lines of longitude, which in reality converge toward the poles, have been straightened, so stretching the areas between them in an east-west direction. To compensate for this, Mercator stretched the parallels of latitude further apart as the poles are approached. The result is the enlarging of the polar areas while preserving the basic shape of the coastlines. The great advantage of the Mercator chart is that a straight line on the chart gives the correct course.

Once this gridwork of latitude and longitude had been developed, it only remained for the chart makers to draw in the coastlines. This proved as difficult as ever, for compasses were so inaccurate, so little was known of variation or deviation, that correct bearings were almost impossible to obtain. Correct distances were likewise difficult to obtain. When these things are taken into account, it really is a wonder

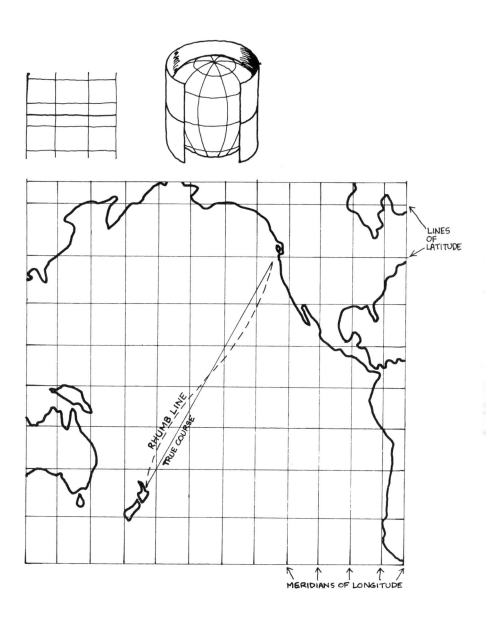

Mercator projection. The lines of latitude are further apart nearer the poles to compensate for the east-west stretching of the Arctic and Antarctic zones. The most useful aspect of the Mercator projection is that a straight line between two points represents the true course. The shortest distance, however, is shown by a curved rhumb line.

that the maps and charts of the medieval mariner show anything barely recognisable.

Because early charts were far from accurate and, until Mercator, difficult to use, many seamen found it easier to use a globe to plot their courses and estimate their positions. They did not have to be particularly good at mathematics if they used a globe. It was in the making of accurate globes that young Gerard Mercator, from Flanders, received his early training; he made globes that were large enough for the navigator to use and yet not too large for convenience. These globes had meridians of longitude and parallels of latitude marked on them, and various scales of distance as many countries of Europe used different units of measurement. Most useful of all, the globes had a flexible band, covering a quarter of a circle, which could be laid in any direction across the surface of the globe to read off the course from one point to another.

But navigators had to wait until 1541 for Mercator's globe and 1585 for Volume I of his 'Atlas'. This was the first time that a collection of maps had been given that particular name.

In the meantime the great age of discovery was dawning. It was time for Diaz, Da Gama, Columbus and Cabot to set sail, and push back the boundaries of the known world.

CHAPTER 5

Indies East and Indies West

Though the Norsemen had sailed across the north Atlantic, when the first Mediterranean sailors left the Straits of Gibraltar they kept close to the land.

By 1420 Prince Henry of Portugal, Henry the Navigator, had gathered round him skilled navigators, masters and pilots, to explore the west coast of Africa. The avowed object was to convert to Christianity the native peoples; the 'River of Gold' in the kingdom of Ghana, ruled by Prester John, would make a welcome addition to Henry's coffers. Fearfully, the ships sailed southwards, close to the land, until they turned back terrified when wind and current started to carry them more quickly away from their homes. Once outside known waters the old methods could no longer help them. The compass only showed them that they were sailing from safety into the danger of the unknown.

Other ships sent out by Henry the Navigator struck out south-west from Portugal and soon discovered Madeira and even the Azores. The winds were favourable; during the summer they blew from the north-east, but as winter approached they swung round and blew from the south-west —back to Portugal.

It was on the return voyages that the pilot had to be most careful in judging how far they had sailed, so that the ships would not come close to land during the hours of darkness. All pilots over-estimated their speeds so that the look-out would be on his guard. This practice of over-estimating proved to be very awkward for Christopher Columbus.

Christopher Columbus (1451–1506).

Cristobal Colon, or Cristoforo Colombo, was born in Genoa in 1451, the son of a wool weaver. His older brothers went to sea and so did Christopher. He sailed north, perhaps as far as Iceland, and south as far as Guinea and the Gold Coast in 1482. On every voyage he measured the altitude of the sun and wrote his findings in the margin of a book of navigation:

'We may therefore say that the circumference of the earth at the equator is 20,400 miles, and likewise that Master Yosepius, the physician and astrologer, found it to be the same...'

As Marco Polo had walked to China, men knew how far that was, and if the circumference at the Equator was only 20,400 miles then the distance across the ocean to the west would be quite small. But Columbus had to persuade a monarch to provide ships and stores and persuade a crew that they would not fall over the edge of the world. He asked the King of Portugal for ships, but as Bartolomeo Diaz had already sailed round the southernmost tip of Africa, Portugal had her way to the Indies. He asked Henry VII of England; Christopher's brother travelled to the English Court to present his case but Henry thought him mad. He considered

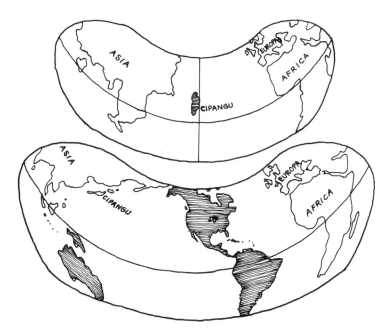

In Columbus' time 1° at the Equator was thought to equal 56 miles. Columbus therefore estimated the earth's circumference as 20,400 miles, and so hoped to reach the Indies in a mere nine weeks.

asking Charles VIII of France, but before he could travel to the French Court he was summoned to the Court of Ferdinand and Isabella of Spain. On April 17th 1492 . . .

'Your Highnesses, as true Sovereigns of the said Ocean, henceforth appoint the said Cristoval Colon, in all those islands and mainlands which by his labour and industry shall be discovered or acquired in the said Ocean, Admiral during his life, and after his death his heirs and successors, from one to the other perpetually . . .'

He set out from Palos on August 3rd 1492, with his three ships, *Santa Maria, Niña* and *Pinta*. By the 8th the *Pinta* was so badly damaged that it took nearly three weeks in the Canary Isles to make her seaworthy again. The crossing of the Atlantic started on 1st September and Christopher Columbus began to deceive his crew. In his Journal, as retold by Bartolome de Las Casas, we find written:

'Sunday, September 9th
He made 15 leagues that day and decided to reckon less than he had made, so that the crews should not lose heart or be alarmed if the voyage grew long. That night he made 120 Roman miles at 10 Roman miles an hour, 30 leagues in all. The sailors steered badly . . . for which the Admiral rebuked them many times.

'Monday, September 17
. . . they saw much more seaweed . . . and in this they found a live crab, which the Admiral kept, because crabs are not found more than 80 leagues from the land. The water of the sea was now less salt . . . and the breezes even gentler. All were much gladdened . . . and whichever ship was speediest forged on ahead in the hope of sighting land before the others.'

October 12th 1492

But at night they huddled together with a light hung from each stern so that they would not be separated in the dark. They had to sail on until October 11 before they saw any true signs of land—a reed, a stick which seemed to have been cut with a knife, a small plank and a twig with roses growing on it. On October 12 Columbus set foot on San Salvador in the Bahamas, believing that he had reached the Indies. Not until Magellan's ships actually reached the Indies after crossing the Pacific was the true distance discovered, and by then Columbus had been dead for sixteen years.

The sun would be either due North or South at noon. By taking its compass bearing, therefore, the compass could be checked.

Judging speed and distance was part of every sailor's duties, but was the special responsibility of the pilot. Judgement was based on experience; the feel of wind and sea, the motion of the ship all helped, but it was not an accurate method. It was really no more than guesswork. A following current could set the ship far ahead of her estimated position without the pilot being aware of it until the coastline unexpectedly appeared ahead. A head current could alarm the crew by making the voyage last longer than expected. The simple Dutchman's log technique was not used until the 1600s and actually came after the development of the log and line method of measuring speed at sea.

The captains of Columbus' fleets could never agree as to how many miles they had sailed and they had little to help them navigate except a compass; and that needed constant checking against the Pole Star—Stella Maris. The Pole Star was further from the Pole in 1492 and could only indicate

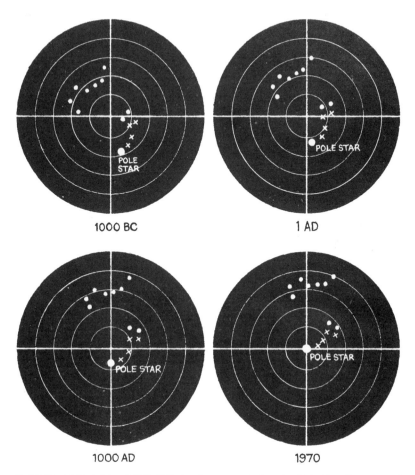

| 1000 BC | 1 AD |
| 1000 AD | 1970 |

Over the period from 1000 B.C. to the present day the Pole Star has moved nearer to the celestial pole. In 3000 B.C. Draconis was the Pole Star, and by A.D. 7500 Alpha Cephei will be the new Pole Star.

true north at certain times. How did you tell which was the 'correct' time when there were no accurate clocks? The sailors 'imagined' a human figure in the sky with the Pole Star at his navel. By noting the position of the two stars known as the 'guards' they could tell the time and whether the Pole Star was due north; but before they could do this they had to memorise the position of the guards at midnight for every two weeks of the year!

The compass that Columbus carried aboard the *Santa Maria* was a much more precise instrument than the needle floated in a straw that had to be stroked with the near magical lodestone. The instrument makers had pivoted the needle, drawn out an accurate wind-rose and enclosed it all within a small box for protection. By placing the compass card on top of the needle the pilot was able to allow for the fact that the needle would indicate magnetic north, for by

The compass.

twisting the card he could ensure that it pointed to Stella Maris. To stop the needle from swinging too violently as the ship moved the compass was mounted in gimbals which allowed it to remain level whilst the ship moved about it. Today we fill the compass bowl with alcohol, which will not freeze in cold weather, and with the same gimbals the needle will remain steady in the roughest weather.

Most of the sailors who sailed with the great explorers could neither read nor write, and so a way was devised for them to show how far and in what direction they had sailed during their watch. The device was the traverse board.

The circular section showed a compass rose with eight holes bored along each point of the compass, and each hole

A traverse board. The National Maritime Museum, London.

represented half-an-hour. The helmsman would note the
direction of the wind during the first half-hour of his watch,
let us say it was SW. He would then put a pin in the first
hole of the SW arm. If the wind swung to the NW during
the next half-hour the second pin would go in the second
hole of the NW arm and so on until the four-hour watch

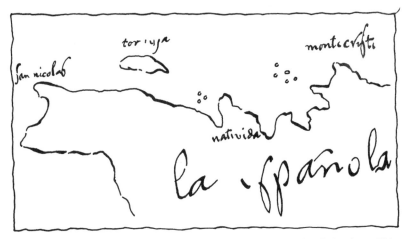

The only sketch map, so far discovered, actually drawn by Columbus. This shows the north-west coast of Hispaniola. Drawn from the original, which is in the Duke of Alba's Archive, Madrid.

was finished, and the pilot would estimate the course made good in that time. The section below the compass rose was a rough guide as to how far the ship sailed each watch. Again a pin was used for each half-hour and put in the hole that showed the speed at which the ship had been sailing.

Judging the speed was very rough and ready, until the middle of the 1500s, when the log and line was developed. A board, weighted at one edge and attached to a long thin line, was thrown over the side, and once well clear of the ship the sand glass was turned, whilst the line attached to the board was allowed to run out quite freely. At the end of the half-minute the line was stopped with a jerk and the board was hauled in. The length of line run out was the distance sailed in 30 seconds. As the mile was considered to contain only 5,000 feet, the line was knotted at 42-foot intervals and remained at that for nearly two hundred years after it was found that the nautical mile was more than 6,000 feet.

Columbus had only one reliable method of finding longitude. This was by observing the position of certain planets and noting the local time that they passed behind the moon.

The times when this occurred were known and had been recorded at Spanish observatories. By comparing local, or ship's time with the recorded time, Columbus could determine his longitude. However, the moon did not often pass conveniently in front of a planet; one cloud might ruin his efforts and another 'eclipse' might not occur for a month.

There were two reliable ways of finding latitude. The first was to measure the angle between the Pole Star and the horizon; accurately observed at the correct time this method gave the navigator his latitude to within twenty miles. The second method was to measure the elevation or angle of the sun above the horizon at mid-day. The navigator then studied his tables to find the sun's declination, how far

The kamal in use. The small rectangle was held out and the distance from the eye was measured by a knotted string held in the mouth. By sailing North or South until a particular star appeared over the horizon, the Arab navigator could estimate his latitude and then sail East or West to reach his destination.

north or south of the Equator it was on that particular day at that particular minute, performed a simple addition or subtraction and found his latitude to within twenty miles.

The instruments developed to measure the altitude of sun or star varied from the simple Arab kamal to the elaborate backstaff.

The kamal was a small rectangle of wood. From a hole in the centre protruded a length of cord. The kamal was held in one hand with the string passing through the mouth. The kamal was moved so that it exactly filled the angle between star and horizon. The length of string was gauged

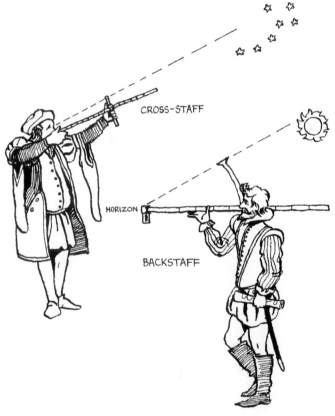

The cross staff could be used for sun, moon or star, the back staff for the sun and a very bright moon.

by a series of knots, the shorter the string the greater the angle.

The cross-staff was an improvement on the kamal, the angle being found by moving the cross-piece along the staff.

The backstaff was a great improvement on both kamal and cross-staff. No longer did the navigator have to squint into the sun. His task was to bring the shadow of the vane on to the slit made in the small plate fixed at the end of the staff.

The seaman's astrolabe could measure angles to a fine degree of accuracy in calm weather, but was almost impossible to use when there were even the smallest waves. Then its accuracy was only within 5–6° or about 300 miles. To use the instrument the pilot usually anchored and rowed ashore.

In all this time little was done in England to master and improve the new methods of navigation. It is believed that

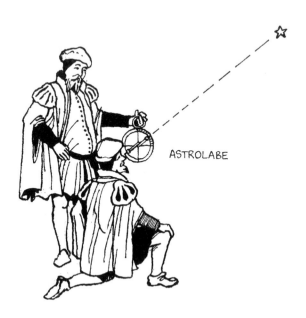

ASTROLABE

The astrolabe needed two people for moon and star sights, one to hold and read the scale, the other to sight *up* through the two small holes.

A mariner's astrolabe, c. 1585. National Maritime Museum, London.

few English seamen even used charts until they were introduced following John Cabot's discovery of Newfoundland
in 1497. Cabot sailed from Bristol, then one of the leading
ports and second only to London in later years, on 2nd May.
His small ship, the *Matthew*, with a crew of 18, sailed to
the west to discover a northern route to Cathay. After seven

weeks he reached Newfoundland, landed in Nova Scotia and then was forced to return as his supplies were running short. For his discovery he was rewarded with £10 by Henry VII.

A second voyage by Sebastian Cabot, son of John Cabot, again failed to find a sea route to the Indies, but he brought back word of the shallow fishing grounds off Newfoundland where cod were so plentiful that they could be hauled up by the bucketful.

John and Sebastian Cabot used globes to draw in the lands which they had discovered for the English Crown. Sebastian made the first real contribution to the scientific training of navigators in England. After serving for some time as Pilot-Major to the Spanish Crown, he was happy

A navigation school in the 1600s. The National Maritime Museum, London.

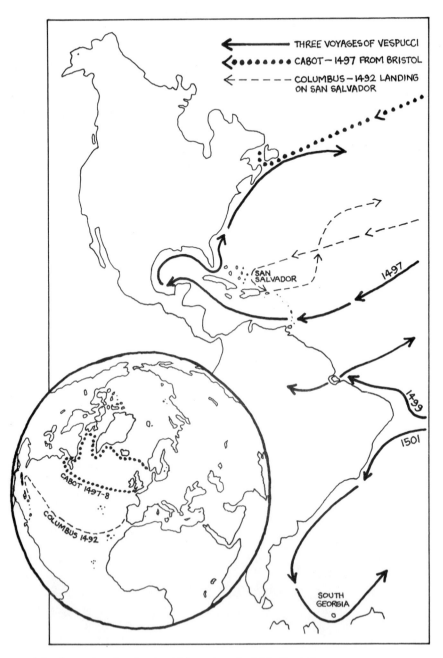

THREE VOYAGES OF VESPUCCI
CABOT — 1497 FROM BRISTOL
COLUMBUS — 1492 LANDING ON SAN SALVADOR

SAN SALVADOR

1497

1499

1501

SOUTH GEORGIA

CABOT 1497-8
COLUMBUS 1492

Atlantic exploration in the 15th and early 16th Centuries.

to make England his home 'for a large sum of money', and to bring with him the knowledge and skill of the Mediterranean navigators. Within one year Sebastian had organised a training ship, taking 70 young men as well as boys; all later became ships' captains. They cruised as far as the eastern Mediterranean and back, learning their navigation from a Spanish pilot called Nobiezia from Cadiz.

One of the young men on that first training cruise was Richard Chancellor, who later sailed with Sir Hugh Willoughby to the Arctic and the White Sea. Chancellor survived when the rest of the expedition were frozen to death and he made his way to Moscow. Thus began the Muscovy Company in 1555 and trade with Russia.

Stephen Borough was the chief pilot, and he trained masters and pilots who worked for the company. Borough had seen the Spanish navigation schools and returned to England determined to organise schools along similar lines. But he found many difficulties to overcome. He could not find staff for his school, for those who knew more than the average pilot would not teach others for fear of losing their own living, and many were ashamed to admit that they needed to learn anything more.

With the opening of the New World to the West and the expansion of the Old World to the East, England had to master the art and science of navigation if she hoped to keep abreast of Spain and Portugal.

CHAPTER 6

All the way round

Columbus died believing that he had discovered Asia by sailing westwards. Amerigo Vespucci, if his accounts are to be believed, actually landed in Nova Scotia 18 days before Cabot, having sailed through the Gulf of Mexico and coasted northwards before using the westerlies to take him back to Spain. In 1499 he sailed up the Amazon and two years later sailed south as far as the Antarctic, meeting with icebergs and even sighting the islands of South Georgia. A chart maker, who translated Vespucci's journals, suggested that the continents be named America after him. But Amerigo Vespucci never found the route to the Pacific: neither did the Cabots who sought a North-West Passage.

However, in 1519, Ferdinand Magellan with five ships and 268 men left Cadiz, sailing westwards to reach the Moluccas, the Spice Islands. The Emperor, Charles V, was so impressed by his arguments that he granted Magellan the right to one-fifteenth share of the profits from any island of his choosing once he had discovered more than six islands. This would be a fortune indeed. The little fleet comprised the *San Antonio* (120 tons), *Trinidad* (110 tons), *Concepçion* (90 tons), *Victoria* (85 tons) and *Santiago* (75 tons), Magellan himself sailing in the *Trinidad*.

Magellan was Portuguese; he had served Portugal well for many years. He dropped from royal favour when a false charge was brought against him accusing him of 'losing' some captured horses and cattle. He hastened to Lisbon to put his case before the King, but his enemies had first word

A page from the journal of Antonio Pigafetta. Courtesy of Biblioteca Ambrosiana, Milan.

and Magellan was refused an audience. So after thirteen years' service to Portugal he was told he was not wanted. However, when he took service with Charles V of Spain, the Portuguese first tried to stop the fleet from sailing and then bribed certain of the captains to cause trouble. They were happy to take the bribes and boasted that if Magellan made a wrong move they would kill him. This would then allow the glory of the expedition and the fruits of its success to be reaped by them. Forewarned is forearmed; whilst the fleet was anchored at Teneriffe in the Canaries, a swift caravel from Spain brought a warning to Magellan from his father-in-law that the ringleader was Juan de Cartagena who commanded the *San Antonio*.

We have an almost complete account of the voyage from the diary kept by Antonio Pigafetta, a young Italian who sailed with Magellan, and there are detailed lists of the stores and cargo carried by the ships. For navigation they carried:

24	parchment charts	6	pairs of compasses
21	wooden quadrants	7	astrolabes
35	compass needles	18	hour glasses

and

Ruy Falerio's treatise on the art of finding Latitude.

(Falerio himself was to have gone with Magellan but changed his mind when an astrological prediction foretold the voyage to be doomed.)

Ships' stores for the voyage included:

biscuits	wine
olive oil	anchovies
dried pork	cheeses
sugar	medicines

whilst the armoury was packed to bursting with:

1,000	lances	1,000	boarding pikes
10	dozen javelins	95	dozen darts
60	crossbows	360	dozen arrows

and sundry swords

and for trade with the natives:

cloth	caps
kerchiefs	combs
mirrors	brass basins
knives, scissors	fish-hooks

500 lb. of crystals 'which are diamonds of all colours'
and
20,000 small bells of three kinds.

With fair winds the fleet reached Cape Verde, for they were in the belt of the NE trade winds, but then instead of sailing to the south, Magellan reached the Equator and then tried to sail west along it. For sixty days they encountered the calms, head winds, storms and torrential rains of the doldrums. Pigafetta wrote:

'In these tempests, the "corpo santo", or St. Elmo's fire, often appeared, and in one which we experienced on a certain very dark night it showed itself at the summit of the main-mast with such brightness that it seemed like a burning torch, remaining there for the space of more than two hours...'

The fleet began to run short of provisions, and quarrels sprang up between Magellan and the other captains. More and more often Juan de Cartagena disobeyed Magellan's orders and one day he openly scoffed and sneered at Magellan's navigation and his choice of course. (If Magellan had sailed further south he would have picked up the SE Trades that would have taken him across the Atlantic in 20–30 days with fair skies and a steady wind.) De Cartagena was arrested.

Eventually, the fleet reached South America and, coasting southwards, found a sheltered inlet in which to pass the winter; but they were put on reduced rations, which once more stirred up trouble. On Easter Day only the new captain of the *San Antonio* accepted Magellan's invitation to dine. The remainder captured the *San Antonio*, intending to sail back to Spain. Magellan dealt harshly with the traitors; de Cartagena and a priest were marooned, one captain was killed in the fighting, another died from his wounds and a third was beheaded. For the time being the mutiny was crushed.

The fleet waited from Easter until October 18th for warmer weather before continuing the voyage south. Two ships sailed ahead into a likely opening and three days later

FERDINANDES MAGALANES LVSITANVS *anfractuoso curiyo fuperato, ꝗ̃ tellari ad Auftrum nomen dedit, cuifque navis omnium prima atque noviffima Solis curfum in terris emulata; terra totius globum circumit. An. Sal. ꝏ.D.XXII.*

Ferdinand Magellan (1480–1521) entering the Pacific Ocean. Engraving by Stradanus. The National Maritime Museum, London.

returned reporting a wide, deep passage. Whilst the ships were divided those on the *San Antonio* slipped away and sailed back to Spain. One month after entering the narrow strait, the fleet, reduced to three (the *Santiago* had been wrecked), came to the end of the 320-mile voyage from the Atlantic to the peaceful and calm Pacific Ocean. Now every mile to the north-west would surely bring them within sight of the Moluccas! They had no idea of the immensity of the ocean they were crossing. Supplies ran short:

'Such a dearth of bread and water was there that we ate by ounces and held our noses as we drank the water from the stench of it . . . We ate biscuit, but in truth it was biscuit no longer but a powder full of worms . . . and in addition it was stinking with the urine of rats . . . [We were forced to eat] the hides covering the main yards; these, exposed to the sun and rain and wind, had become so hard that we were forced first to soften them by putting them overboard for four or five days. We were also forced to eat the sawdust of wood, and rats, which became such a delicacy that we paid half a ducat apiece for them.'

After ninety-eight days they came to the Marianas, and rested and fed for three days and tried to stop the natives from stealing everything they touched. The islands were immediately named the Ladrones (Thieves) Islands and kept that name for many years. The fleet sailed on to Cebu, where the Rajah was so impressed with the might and power of Spain that a treaty was made between them. To help Spain's new ally Magellan agreed to help the Rajah by attacking the nearby island of Mactan. With fifty men Magellan set fire to the main village only to find himself surrounded.

'Thus we fought for an hour or more,' Pigafetta writes, 'until at length an Indian succeeded in wounding the Captain in the face with a bamboo spear. He, being desperate, plunged his lance in the Indian's breast, leaving it there. But, wishing to use his sword, he could only draw it half-way from the sheath because of a spear wound he had received in his right arm. Seeing this, the enemy all rushed at him; and one of them with a long terzado, like a large scimitar, gave him a heavy blow of the left leg, which caused him to fall forward on his face. Then the Indians threw themselves upon him with iron-pointed bamboo spears, and every weapon they had, and ran him through—our mirror, our light, our comforter, our true guide—until they killed him.'

More of the men were later killed by the Rajah himself and only two ships continued the voyage. One ship alone returned to Spain, the little *Victoria,* manned by 47 of the 268 that had set out in 1519. On 8th September 1522 they reached Seville. Oddly enough the first man to circum-navigate the globe was Magellan's slave who came originally from the Moluccas and so completed the round trip when the small fleet arrived in Tidore.

The *Victoria* was commanded by Sebastian del Cano who was one of the Easter Day mutineers whom Magellan had spared; in the first flush of excitement he was heaped with honours and Magellan was forgotten.

The *Trinidad* tried to return to Spain by sailing back across the Pacific, but was forced back by contrary winds, and captured by the Portuguese, and only a few of her crew managed to make their way back to Spain years later.

Sir Francis Drake's voyage around the world began very much as a cloak and dagger mystery. Only the Queen, by whose command and permission the raiding voyage was made, and her secretary, Sir Francis Walsingham, knew that Drake was to raid the Spanish colonies on the west coast of South America. Secrecy was all-important, for England and Spain were not officially at war and there were attempts being made to patch up a peace between Philip of Spain and Elizabeth of England. But Spain had treated English seamen badly. 'I would gladly be revenged on the King of Spain for divers injuries that I have received,' said Elizabeth to Drake, but it must be done quietly '. . . and of all men my Lord Treasurer (Lord Burghley) is not to know it.' So Drake prepared his expedition with three different objectives:

1. The secret raiding of Spanish settlements.

2. A voyage to discover, if possible, Terra Australis Incognita, believed to contain more gold and jewels than South America. (This was told to officers only.)

3. A voyage to Alexandria to open up the spice trade. (Public announcement.)

In some ways Drake's voyage was similar to Magellan's. By the time his fleet reached Port St. Julian Drake had to deal with mutiny by one Thomas Doughty, his personal friend. With so much at stake Drake could not afford to be merciful. Doughty was tried and condemned. Before his execution he took his last meal with Drake and together they received the Sacrament. Then Doughty was beheaded.

On the shore they found rotting timber they believed to have been the gallows where, sixty years before, Magellan had also dealt out rough justice to traitors.

Drake soon took full command of his small fleet and let it be known that they were to raid the Spanish settlements on the west coast of South America. Drake chose to take the inside passage through the Strait of Magellan rather than risk the uncertainty of Cape Horn, for though the Vaz Duardo map of 1568 shows no sign of the mysterious Terra Australis, many believed that Tierra del Fuego was joined to it. Drake negotiated the narrow, winding, rock-studded passage in sixteen days, but once clear he was driven far to the south and yet found no sign of the southern continent. During these gales all three ships were separated, the *Marigold* was never seen again, whilst the *Elizabeth* was sailed back to England. The *Golden Hind* sailed north, attacking

Drake's plate of brass. Reproduced by permission of The Director, The Bancroft Library, University of California, Berkeley, California.

settlements and taking the Spanish treasure ship *Cacafuego*. Taking the treasure, Drake released his prisoners and let it be known that he would return to England by crossing the Pacific. The Spaniards thought of course that he fully intended to make further attacks on their possessions and all their efforts to find him near Panama failed.

He sailed north towards California and searched out a sheltered inlet where he could safely refit the badly strained and leaking *Golden Hind*. There is no surviving record of just where he refitted; he named the region New Albion and set up on a post a plate of brass with an inscription that claimed the land for the Queen of England. In 1936 a motorist, parked on the verge of the highway, found a brass plate. Inscribed in English of a style and spelling definitely Elizabethan, the wording runs:

'Bee it knowne vnto all men by these presents ivne. 17.1579

'By the Grace of God and in the name of Herr Maiesty Qveen Elizabeth of England and herr svccessors forever I take possession of this Kingdome whose King and people freely resigne their right and title in the whole land vnto Herr Maiesties keeping now named by me an to be knowne vnto all men as Nova Albion.

'G. Francis Drake
'Hole for sixpence.'

Drake sailed from New Albion in July 1579 with a full set of Pacific charts and sailing instructions, captured from an otherwise empty ship. But the charts were a valuable prize in themselves. It took three months to sail across the Pacific and reach the Moluccas where Drake took on a cargo of six tons of spices, almost as valuable as six tons of gold or silver. Leaving the Moluccas the *Golden Hind* struck a reef before she reached the open waters of the Indian Ocean. She stuck fast. Guns were thrown overboard, shot too; anything not essential went over. Still she stuck. Reluctantly

Drake ordered some of the valuable spices to be jettisoned and she floated. The gold and silver stayed safely below.

After a voyage reaching across three oceans and lasting for three years Drake reached Plymouth Sound on September 26th 1580. His first question was whether the Queen was alive and well. If she were dead, then England and Spain might be allied and he might be hanged for a pirate. But Elizabeth was very much alive and though Spain demanded the return of the treasure and the death of Drake, Elizabeth gave them neither.

Drake made great use of sailing directions which were known as rutters from the French word 'Routier'. The 'Book of the Sea Carte', published in the 1590s, contains sailing directions, such as those for entering Falmouth, which are quite sufficient for making a safe entry today:

'To enter Falmouth ye shall fynde a rocke in the myddle of the entryinge, leve it on the larborde syde and go towarde east by those and when ye be past it go streight in for the baye is . . . large, anker where ye will at 5 or 6 fadoms amyd the baye and if ye will go at the tournynge of the full sea . . . there is a banke to passe which ye shall finde at lowe water at two fadoms and a halfe.

'From Dodman to the Lizarde—one kennynge and three mile.'

A kenne was an early measure of distance and meant that two points were just within sight of one another on a clear day, that is about twenty miles apart. Drake, of course, prepared rutters so that English ships could easily locate Spanish ports in order to harass Spain's preparations for the Armada. Outline sketches of hills, headlands and bays made it easier to recognise sectors of the coastline. To make these small sketches each expedition carried a draughtsman and at the foot of one small sketch of an island in the West Indies made on a later voyage is this sad footnote:

'This morninge when the discription noted or taken of this Lande beinge the 28 of Januarie 1595 beinge wedens daie in the morninge. Sr Frauncis Dracke Died of the bludie flix righte of the Ilande de Buena Ventura, som 6 Leagues at see whom now resteth with the Lorde.'

CHAPTER 7

Time is longitude and longitude is time

For nearly two hundred years after Magellan's single surviving ship, the *Victoria*, completed the first circumnavigation of the globe the whole problem of how to find correct longitude was a puzzle and a danger to seamen. However in 1522, the year that the *Victoria* returned, Gemma Frisius, Mercator's teacher, proposed that accurate clocks be taken to sea to find out the ship's longitude by comparing the time difference between noon by the sun (i.e. when it appeared highest in the sky) and the time shown by the clock. It took the next two hundred years to develop a clock that was sufficiently accurate!

In 1555 William Borough tested the idea but the watches and clocks were wildly inaccurate—sometimes gaining, sometimes losing up to fifteen minutes a day. This would mean that a ship's position would be out by as much as 250 miles in a single day. So difficult was the problem of accuracy that the astronomers sought other ways to find longitude at sea. The clock makers could hardly be blamed. Firstly they had to contend with the wild motion of a small ship in a heavy sea. Any clock that needed a pendulum to regulate its motion was bound to be inaccurate. Springs of steel were as unreliable as the steel, whilst oil used to lubricate the delicate mechanism became thick and congealed in the cold, slowing the clock, but became thin and even evaporated in the heat of the tropics. It was another side of the problem of temperature that formed one of the most difficult problems in the making of an accurate clock or watch. Whatever metal

69

A nocturnal. The notched edge meant that the time could be 'felt' in the dark. Crown copyright. Science Museum, London.

was used it would expand and contract as the temperature changed; if a pendulum increased in length then the swing became slower; if the balance wheel in a watch expanded it too would oscillate more slowly; if cooled it would contract and oscillate more quickly and the watch's rate would vary with the climate. These were the problems facing the clock makers of the time.

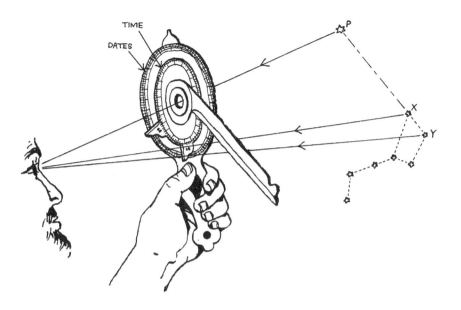

Using a nocturnal.

Meanwhile, finding time at sea was still a matter of observing the sun and stars, finding noon when the sun was at its highest, whilst at night almost any hour could be gauged by using a *nocturnal*. This was a very early form of the circular slide rule. The navigator first set the nocturnal by twisting the inner circle so that the edge of one of the 'ears' crossed the outer circle at that day's date. One 'ear' was for the Little Bear constellation, the other if the Great Bear was to be observed. Then the navigator sighted the Pole Star through the central hole and rotated the long arm so that it lay along the two pointers of the Plough. When this was done the time could be read where the long arm crossed the inner circle. This gave the local or ship's time to within five or ten minutes.

Some of the curious ways in which men tried to find out their longitude were of very doubtful value. One proposal was for a large hour glass that was to be turned every twenty-four hours—again the heat of the tropics would enlarge the small hole allowing the sand to run faster, whilst the slightest moisture reaching the sand in humid tropical climates would make it run slowly. Some even proposed that ships should carry water clocks. The more scientifically minded, realising that the magnetic pole did not coincide with the true pole, suggested that longitude could be found where a line of magnetic variation crossed a parallel of latitude, whilst Henry Bond claimed that by using a compass needle pivoted so that it swung up and down (dip needle) he could determine longitude.

It was the invention of the telescope by Hans Lippersheim in 1608 that eventually led the way to more accurate star observation and cataloguing and hence more accurate navigation at sea.

Charles II did much to further the cause of English navigation. In 1675 he founded the Royal Observatory at Greenwich, appointing a young clergyman, John Flamsteed, as Astronomer Royal. John Flamsteed spent his entire working life cataloguing the 'fixed stars', observing the moon's

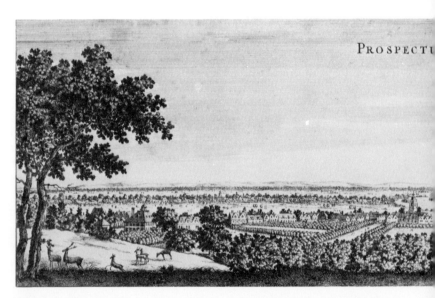

Greenwich Observatory – an early picture. The National Maritime Museum.

movements and so predicting the tides. The French, not to be outdone, established the Paris Observatory. Charles also set up at Christ's Hospital a mathematical school for 40 boys. Isaac Newton wrote:

> 'Whereas the Mathematicall children, being the flower of the Hospitall, are capable of much better learning, and when well instructed and bound out to skilful Masters may in time furnish the Nation with a more skilful sort of Sailors, builders of Ships, Architects . . . than France can ever boast of.'

Astronomers, now equipped with more powerful telescopes, began to discover more about the stars and planets. The Italian, Galileo Galilei, had proposed a method for finding longitude some seventy years before Flamsteed started his work, but the mounting of his telescope was too crude to give sensible results. The method used was to time the eclipses of the four known moons of Jupiter. Telescopes then were not powerful enough to see the nine moons that we now

know revolve around Jupiter. The theory was quite simple; tables giving the time of eclipse for every day of the year for a particular spot were needed; the navigator would note the local or 'ship's' time (i.e. the number of hours and minutes since the sun was on the meridian). The difference between the two times would be the longitude. In practice it proved impossible. The slightest movement of the ship made it impossible to hold the planet and its satellites in view. Furthermore, not all telescopes were as carefully made as Galileo's; most were made from a tube of papiermâché covered with leather, and were very long and unwieldy, hardly strong enough or suitable for use on board ship.

Jupiter's moons. By timing the eclipses of these moons, navigators hoped to be able to find their longitude. The National Maritime Museum, London.

One discovery that came from the study of Jupiter's moons was that light travelled at a set speed. Up until Olaus Römer's discovery it had been believed that light 'travelled' instantaneously from the sun and stars, from candles, fire and other sources of light. Now the astronomers noted that

A telescope *c.* 1646. The National Maritime Museum, London.

at certain times the predicted eclipses of Jupiter's moons were a second or more late. This was found to coincide with the period during which Jupiter's orbit carried the planet much further from the earth. But none of this helped the navigator to establish his longitude. The ten-foot telescopes like Galileo's were completely unmanageable on the deck of a rolling ship.

Next came the reflecting telescope developed by Isaac Newton. This depended upon an accurately ground glass that was then silvered. This type of telescope was only two feet long but it was still impossible to train it on the distant Jupiter moons with sufficient accuracy from the deck of a ship. They even tried to take sights from a heavy chair suspended from above, so that though the ship moved the chair would remain stationary, but with no greater success. After all their experiments there remained but one way—to develop a really accurate clock.

The loss of Sir Cloudesley Shovell's fleet on the rock of the Scillies. The National Maritime Museum, London.

The year 1707 brought disaster to the English Fleet under the command of Sir Cloudesley Shovell. In a heavy westerly gale the fleet ran aground on the rocks of the Scillies and more than 2,000 men were drowned and four ships were lost. The fleet was returning from the Mediterranean where it had taken part in the siege of Toulon. The voyage north had been quite uneventful, but fog closed in once the fleet had come into soundings. The Admiral's ship, the *Association,* struck on the Bishop and Clerk. Sir Cloudesley managed to reach shore alive in Porthellick Cove but a woman on the shore killed him for the sake of his emerald ring. If the Admiral had known his longitude the disaster would not have occurred.

Seven years after this loss the 'Board of Longitude' was set up and a prize of £20,000 was offered to the person who perfected an accurate and practical method of finding longitude at sea. This huge sum, more valuable then than now, showed how important the task of finding an answer to the problem seemed to the Government of the time. Of course there were many ridiculous suggestions; some suggested flashing time signals on the base of clouds, others that the height of the tide, measured by a barometer in the open sea, could be used to tell the time; and from the time, the longitude!

In 1729, John Harrison, son of a Yorkshire carpenter, began work on his first marine clock. Harrison, who had a mathematical streak, worked for a time as a surveyor, then moved to London and became a self-taught clock maker. His reputation grew when it was found that his pendulum clocks neither lost nor gained a single second in a month. He solved the problem of the expansion and contraction of the pendulum by developing a 'grid-iron' pendulum, which while allowing the metal to expand did not alter in length. After six years his first marine clock was ready. It looked rather like a lunar landing vehicle with its legs and spheres and selection of dials. This first marine clock was tested on a voyage to Lisbon and back. The Board of Longitude made him a grant of money to continue his work. In the next twenty-five years Harrison made two more clocks but still the Board of Longitude was not fully satisfied. The clocks were rather large and cumbersome, and in 1761, Harrison, now an old man, completed his first watch-styled time-piece.

To earn the prize money the watch had to be tested on a voyage to the West Indies and back. Harrison's son took the chronometer, the name given to an especially accurate clock, to Portsmouth where it was officially timed and set, and placed under lock and key aboard the ship *Deptford*, which was taking the Governor of Jamaica to his post. An astronomer, by the name of Robinson, accompanied the party and it was his task to work out the local time in Jamaica.

During the voyage there was an opportunity to test the new time-piece as the *Deptford* approached Madeira. The ship's navigators ordered a change of course to reach the island, for they were to take on supplies of beer, but according to the chronometer no change was necessary. Harrison's son begged Captain Digges to maintain his course until the following morning and the following morning the island hove in sight as predicted. By the time the *Deptford* arrived at Port Royal in Jamaica they had been at sea for 81 days. Robinson, the astronomer, set up his instruments and established the local time. When compared with Harrison's chronometer the difference was only 5.1 seconds in 81 days. Ships that arrived after the *Deptford* were as much as 20 minutes out in their calculations so putting them nearly 350 miles from their correct position. On the return voyage the weather was very rough and the chronometer was firmly screwed to the bulkhead and even so the total error was less than two minutes after the round voyage of 147 days. The terms of the award were that the chronometer should be accurate to within two minutes and Harrison's error was 1 minute $54\frac{1}{2}$ seconds. He claimed his reward of £20,000, but was only granted £2,500. However, the following year Parliament offered him a further £5,000. Harrison demanded a second trial and on a voyage to Barbados and back, lasting 156 days, the chronometer lost a mere 15 seconds. Very grudgingly the Board awarded Harrison another £2,500. Before they would grant him the remainder, he had to explain the full workings of his intricate mechanism. The Astronomer Royal took the chronometer to Greenwich and there for nearly a year he studied and tested it still further. Finally another clock maker, Larkum Kendall by name, was asked to produce an exact replica of Harrison's fourth chronometer and it was this copy that Captain Cook took with him on his second voyage in the *Resolution*.

The object of Cook's first voyage was to take astronomers to the island of Tahiti to observe the 'transit of Venus' for the Royal Society. The transit was similar to an eclipse of the sun except that Venus appears as a small dot passing across the face of the sun.

On the return voyage his secret orders were to explore to the south to discover what he could of the 'Terra Incognita' of the earlier geographers and navigators.

Harrison's four chronometers. The National Maritime Museum, London, on loan from the Ministry of Defence (Navy).

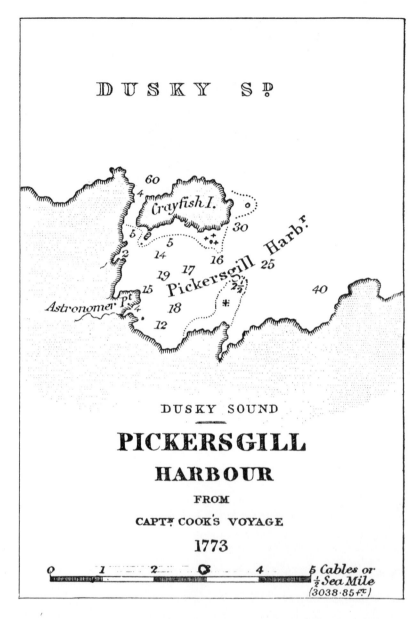

DUSKY SOUND

PICKERSGILL

HARBOUR

FROM

CAPT: COOK'S VOYAGE

1773

Cook's survey work was so accurate that this plan of Pickersgill Harbour, New Zealand, is still used on the up-to-date Admiralty chart. Reproduced from BA chart no. 2589 with the sanction of The Controller, H.M. Stationery Office and of the Hydrographer of the Navy.

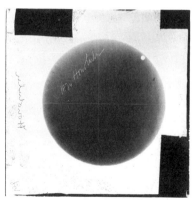
The transit of Venus, 1874.

During this first voyage Cook's method of determining longitude was to measure the angle between moon and sun (or star) and to work out his longitude by referring to his nautical almanac which gave the position of sun and moon in relation to Greenwich. At other times he was able to observe the moons of Jupiter whose movements had by now been accurately predicted as seen from Greenwich.

'29th June
This night Mr Green and I observed an emersion of Jupiter's 1st satellite which happened at 2^h 58' 53" in the A.M. The same emersion happened at Greenwich according to calculation on the 30th at 5^h 17' 43" in the P.M., the difference is 14^h 18' 50" equal to . . . [145° 17' 30" E. of Greenwich.]'

Cook was insistent that an accurate record of the ship's progress be kept at all times and on Tuesday, 11th July, he wrote:

'. . . we were by observation 126° 33' E., the difference of 33' is exactly as the log gave. This however is a degree of accuracy in observation that is seldom to be expected.'

When he set out on his second voyage, the *Resolution* was equipped with four 'watch-machines' and by the time he

The *Resolution* and *Adventure* taking on ice for drinking water, Latitude 61°S Wash drawing by W. Hodges, reproduced by permission of The Mitchell Library, Sydney.

had completed his voyage which lasted from 1772 to 1775 he had proved the worth of Harrison's work in the development of the chronometer.

'On completing the Observations made in this harbour I find the Watch is only $1\frac{2}{3}$ seconds in time different from what it gave last year.'

Cook wrote to the Secretary of the Admiralty:

'Mr. Kendall's Watch (which cost £450) exceeded the expectations of its most zealous advocate and by being now and then corrected by lunar observations has been our faithful guide through all vicissitudes of climates.'

The problem of finding longitude at sea had been solved. But as Isaac Newton is said to have remarked: 'I am not aware that the longitude was ever lost.'

Even though the problem of determining longitude at sea had been solved, there still remained the problem of the point from which longitude should be measured. There was no natural 'middle line' running from north to south from which measurements could be taken and each country measured longitude from within its own boundaries. Only the early Arabs had chosen to measure longitude from the 'Fortunate Isles', the Canaries. Italians based their charts on Rome, the French on Paris, the British on Greenwich. Cardinal Richelieu, in the seventeenth century, proposed that once more longitude should be measured from the meridian passing through the island of Ferro in the Canaries. The French chart makers even complied, but within a few years Ferro was merely marked as being 20° West of Paris!

From the time of Cook's voyages until 1884 each country went its own way until a congress was called in Washington, USA, at which after much argument most countries, excepting France and Brazil, agreed to recognise that the meridian passing through Greenwich was the Prime Meridian from which the rest of the world would measure their longitude. Only in 1911 did France finally adjust her measurements

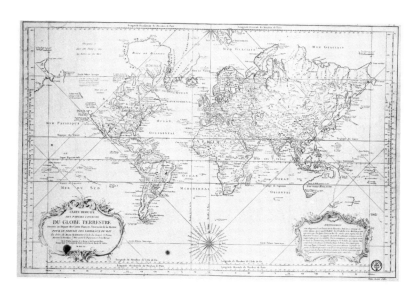

Chart of the world by Bellin Sr., 1755. Note the Prime Meridian drawn through Paris. The National Maritime Museum, London.

and French sailors take their longitude East or West of Greenwich and not Paris.

Captain Cook is known as the Great Navigator, but Edmond Halley is better known for his comet than for the invaluable aid that he gave to seamen by plotting the magnetic variation of the compass for the entire Atlantic Ocean during a voyage made in 1699–1700. From his observations of True North, made from sights taken of stars and planets, he was able to establish the amount by which the compass varied. From his labours came the first isogonic chart that told navigators by how much their compasses

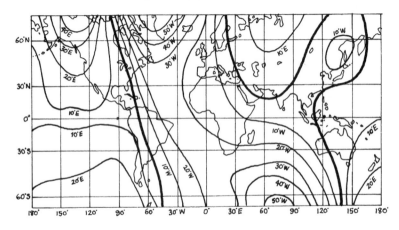

A world isogonic chart showing lines of equal magnetic variation.

varied when sailing either the Atlantic Oceans or the Indian Ocean and beyond to the west coast of Australia and the China Sea. No longer was a prolonged period of cloud such a voyage into the unknown, for at last the compass was a reliable guide.

CHAPTER 8

From Cook to Sumner

From the time of Captain Cook to the coming of the twentieth century there were few major changes in methods of navigation. Instruments were improved and modified with experience; nautical tables, in which the navigator could find the necessary information about the position of the sun, moon and stars for every hour of every day, were made more accurate, charts contained more and more information that could be relied on. However, nothing could be done about bad weather or poor visibility and many fine ships were lost on isolated pinnacles of rock that were uncharted.

Measuring the distance that the ship had run was still a matter of judgement based on 'heaving the log' once every hour. For more than two centuries the log had changed little, still the same triangular piece of wood, still the line with its knots at 42 feet rather than 51 feet, still the half-minute glass. Hauling in the log was made much easier by having one corner fastening held by a light peg pushed into a hole. When the last grain of sand ran through, the jerk of the line being stopped pulled the peg free and allowed the log, held at two points only, to be hauled aboard with ease.

The first major improvement to this system came with the development of the *patent log*. A small brass cylinder, with fins off-set to make it rotate, was towed behind the ship. Each revolution was recorded and a series of clock faces built into the side of the cylinder registered the distance sailed since the log was last read. Though this new log was an improvement on the old system, there were several errors that could creep in. If the ship were travelling fast with a strong following wind, the sudden surges forward would tend to make the log show a greater distance than had actually been sailed. Nor could it record an accurate distance if there was a current flowing; if the current was a helpful one, it was all the more dangerous for the log under-read and you would arrive sooner than expected. If the current was against you then you seemed to sail far further than necessary.

The loss of the *Birkenhead*. She was swept on to an uncharted pinnacle of rock and sank within half an hour.

PEG

LOG CHIP or SHIP

LEAD

LOG CHIP THROWN OVERBOARD.

KNOTS

42 FEET

LOG LINE PAID OUT FREELY FOR 30 SECONDS.

A SHARP TUG FREES AND THE LOG IS EASILY HAULED IN. THE NUMBER OF KNOTS REPRESENTED THE SPEED IN NAUTICAL MILES PER HOUR.

EVEN IN THE 1800'S SEAMEN STILL USED THE SHORT KNOT — 42 FEET, WHICH WAS USED WHEN THE MILE WAS RECKONED AS 5000 FEET,

42 FEET

INSTEAD OF USING THE 51 FEET INTERVAL WHEN THE CORRECT NAUTICAL MILE WAS FOUND TO CONTAIN 6080 FEET AS EARLY AS 1635 BY RICHARD NORWOOD.

51 FEET

Using the log.

An early patent log spinner.

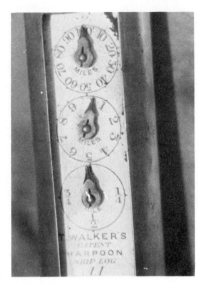

Separate dials give readings to less than ¼ mile.

Nevertheless, it was a great improvement and the later versions of the patent log could be read without hauling in the long length of line. The brass wheel fixed between the line and the recording clock acts as a fly-wheel and tends to even out the surges of speed caused by waves so that a regular speed is recorded. The trouble with towing a log of this design is that fish tend to take it for bait and snap it off. On a modern liner or freighter a patent log is still set when the ship is well clear of congested harbour traffic and the day's run is recorded electronically on the bridge.

Of all the instruments used the sextant is the trademark of the navigator.

Today's sextant is very similar to the instrument presented by John Hadley for the consideration of the Royal Society in 1731. Hadley's octant had a short 45° ($\frac{1}{8}$th of a circle) arc, divided into 90 equal parts each representing 1° of altitude. Later, so that angles of more than 90° could be measured, the length of the arc was increased to 60° ($\frac{1}{6}$th of a circle) and the sextant was born.

This early octant had no telescopes. Sighting was done through a small hole in the vane.

The sextant is based on two very simple laws of optics.

1 *The angle of incidence equals the angle of reflection.*

2 *If a ray of light is reflected between two plane mirrors, the angle between the mirrors is half the angle between the objects observed.*

(In terms of the sextant, this means that if a ray of light from sun, star or moon is reflected from one mirror to another, then the angle between the mirrors is half the angle between the first and last directions of the ray, that is the angle between the heavenly body and the horizon. The halving also accounts for the 60° arc of the sextant being able to measure angles up to 120°.)

To take a sun sight hold the sextant vertically in the right hand. So that your eye will not be damaged by the dazzling reflection a series of shades is provided for each mirror. One or more of these darkened glasses must be pulled into place. Set the index arm at zero and point the telescope straight at the sun. With the index arm at zero, the true sun and reflected sun will appear as one. Next, gradually begin to lower the telescope towards the horizon at the same time moving the index bar forward so that the reflected sun remains in view in the horizon mirror. This requires a steady hand and some practice. When the sun appears to rest on the horizon swing the base of the sextant gently from left to right and back. If the sun appears to swing back and forth evenly this shows that you are holding the sextant in the vertical position. When you are satisfied that your reading is correct, clamp the arm in position and take the reading from the scale marked along the limb of the sextant. Older sextants could be read accurately to the nearest ten seconds of arc (1/360°) by means of a vernier scale which was read through a tiny microscope fitted above it, whereas the modern sextant can be just as accurately read by the figures marked on the large rotating micrometer head by which the final adjustments are made when taking the sight.

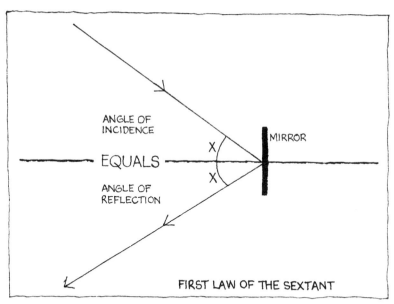

ANGLE OF
INCIDENCE

EQUALS

ANGLE OF
REFLECTION

MIRROR

X

X

FIRST LAW OF THE SEXTANT

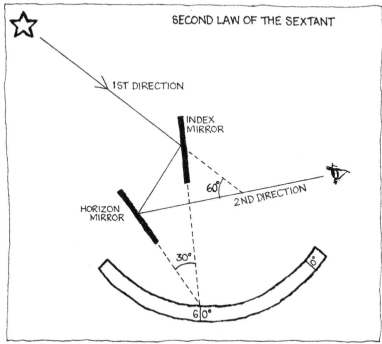

SECOND LAW OF THE SEXTANT

1ST DIRECTION

INDEX
MIRROR

60°

2ND DIRECTION

HORIZON
MIRROR

30°

60°

0°

How the sextant works.

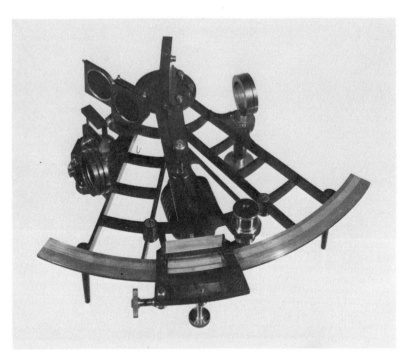

A sextant of the 1890s.

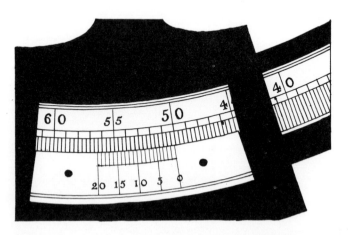

Reading a sextant. It's not quite on 50°; count along the lower lines until two lines, lower and upper, match *exactly* — that's it, number 4. The reading is therefore 50°4'.

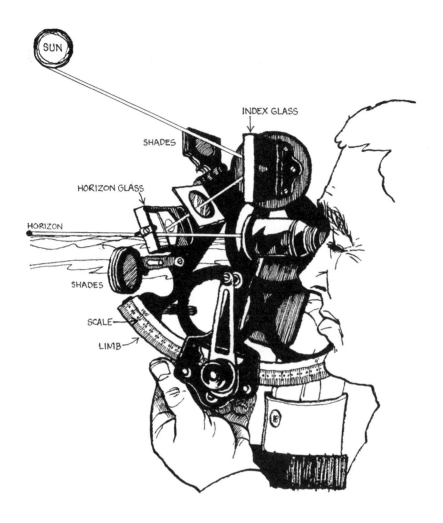

SUN

INDEX GLASS

SHADES

HORIZON GLASS

HORIZON

SHADES

SCALE

LIMB

Taking a sight — or 'shooting' the sun.

By holding the sextant on its side it is possible to measure the angle between two shore objects, or two buoys which would be a first step in fixing the ship's position, but these uses of the sextant belong to pilotage, which is dealt with in a later chapter.

As well as the gradual improvements to instruments there were two developments in methods of plotting the ship's

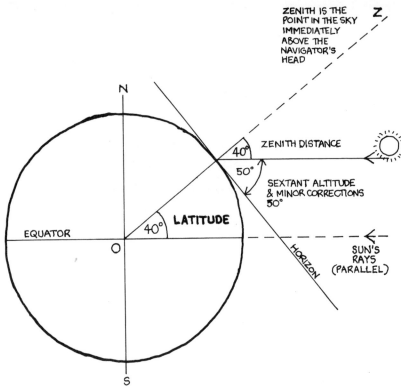

Z

N

40°

ZENITH DISTANCE

50°

SEXTANT ALTITUDE & MINOR CORRECTIONS 50°

LATITUDE

40°

EQUATOR

O

HORIZON

SUN'S RAYS (PARALLEL)

S

Finding latitude by a *meridian altitude*, the noon sight to find the altitude of the sun above.

On March 21st and September 21st (Equinoxes) the sun is vertically above the Equator. It is obvious that, as the rays of light are parallel, the angles they make with ZO must be equal. Thus Zenith Distance is equal to latitude, and Zenith Distance can be found by subtracting the altitude of the sun from 90° — *but only on March 21st and September 21st*. For other days the sun's distance North or South of the Equator (declination) must be found from the *Nautical Almanack* and used.

position at sea by means of sun and star sights. Before 1837 the navigator determined his latitude by taking a sun sight at noon (local or ship's time). By a simple calculation taking only a few seconds he could work out his latitude and then by comparing local time with Greenwich time as shown by his chronometer he readily established his longitude. However the sun does not always oblige the navigator by being visible at noon on the dot. Captain Sumner, an American, was running towards the rocky coast of Ireland in 1837 and

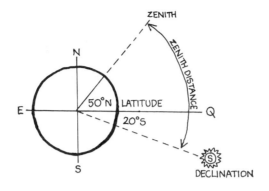

Ship and sun on opposite sides of the Equator.
Latitude = Zenith Distance (70°) − Declination (20°) = 50° N.

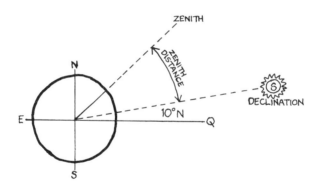

Ship and sun on same side of the Equator.
Latitude = Zenith Distance (40°) + Declination (10°) = 50° N

had been without a sight of the sun for days. But at 10 a.m.
the sun appeared and so he took a quick sight. To complete
his calculations accurately he needed to know his latitude,
but without a sight for so long he had only his dead reckoning
to go by. So by this figure he plotted his position. Then, to
check his figures, he used a different latitude some miles to
the north, and yet a third time even further north of his
assumed position. The three positions all lay along a straight
line which led towards Smalls Light, on the south coast

of Ireland. He altered course slightly to follow the line, and in less than an hour Smalls Light was sighted ahead; Captain Sumner had discovered the Astronomical Position Line. As a result of this discovery navigators are able to make use of sights taken at any hour for either the sun or the stars and by taking two such sights of different stars two circles of position can be plotted. These circles will cross one another at two points and the ship could be at either. However, the two points are usually so far apart that it is perfectly obvious which is the correct position. In the diagram on page 97 no navigator would imagine himself to be off the coast of Ireland if he had only just left Newfoundland, nor believe himself near Newfoundland if he had spent several days crossing the North Atlantic. The whole process was made much more accurate by a Frenchman named Marq St. Hilaire, who has given his name to the present-day method of fixing the ship's position by astronomical position lines.

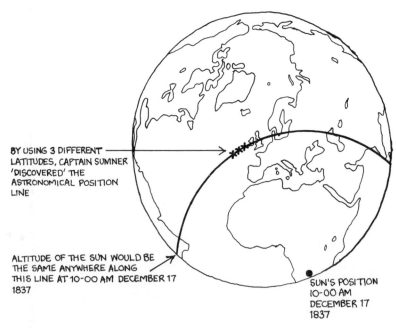

BY USING 3 DIFFERENT LATITUDES, CAPTAIN SUMNER 'DISCOVERED' THE ASTRONOMICAL POSITION LINE

ALTITUDE OF THE SUN WOULD BE THE SAME ANYWHERE ALONG THIS LINE AT 10-00 AM DECEMBER 17 1837

SUN'S POSITION 10-00 AM DECEMBER 17 1837

Captain Sumner's position line.

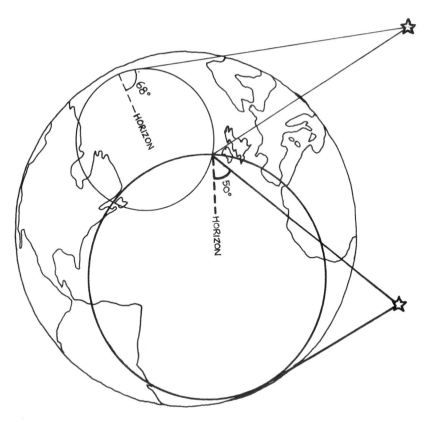

Using two stars, two circles of equal altitude are found. Where they cross at a reasonable point is the ship's position.

CHAPTER 9

Navigation today

Electrical aids to navigation vary from fairly simple echo sounders to very complex Doppler systems that need a computer to unscramble the radio reflections as they are received.

An echo sounder is used to find and record the depth of water below the ship. The speed of sound through water is about 5,000 feet per second. The echo sounder beams a high pitched 'bleep', lasting as little as 1–10 milliseconds, towards the sea-bed. The faint echo of this tiny sound is picked up, amplified or magnified, and operates a pen which moves back and forth across a strip of moving paper, so that a permanent record of the sea floor is obtained.

Asdic works on a similar principle except that the 'ping' is beamed out horizontally beneath the vessel. Travelling at 5,000 feet per second the returning echo quickly pinpoints the distance and bearing of an underwater object, such as a submarine. The skilled operator soon learns to detect and interpret the sounds received and can accurately gauge the speed and course of the other vessel—one of the first practical applications of the 'Doppler Shift'. If you stand at the side of a straight stretch of main road and listen to the noise made by the approach of a car, you will notice that the pitch or note of the engine rises as the vehicle approaches and then drops as it speeds away. Now the car is emitting a regular amount of noise and all the sound waves travel at the same speed, but, because the car is getting closer more sound waves arrive closer together, so the pitch rises. As the car

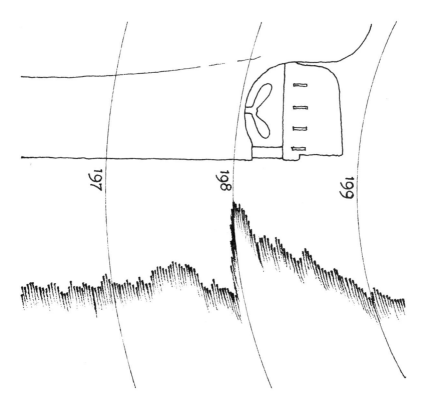

Echo sounding equipment. The trace shows a reef very close to the shore mooring buoy where giant ore tankers load New Zealand ironsand for Japan.

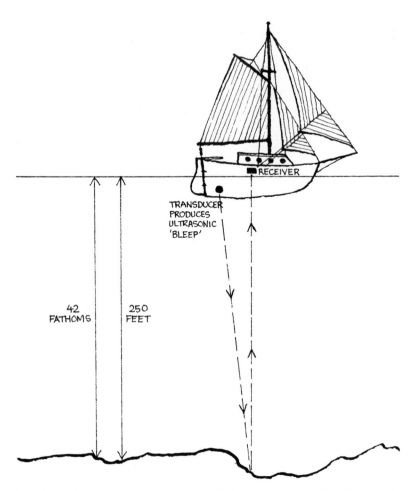

42
FATHOMS

250
FEET

TRANSDUCER
PRODUCES
ULTRASONIC
'BLEEP'

RECEIVER

Sound travels through the water at 5,000 feet per second. The 'bleep' will be echoed and return to the receiver in 1/10 second.

recedes the waves have further to travel and so they arrive at greater intervals, making the pitch lower. Asdic operators soon learn to read the echoes; if the other vessel is going away the echo of the 'ping' will be longer than the original sound, whereas if it is approaching the echo will be shorter. Asdic is, of course, essential in navigating submarines under water where obstacles on the sea-bed must be detected and avoided.

Sound waves 'bunch up' on each other as submarine approaches and pitch rises

Ping Ping Ping Ping Ping

Ping Ping Ping Piinng

Piiinng

Sound waves spread as submarine departs and 'pitch' falls

Sound waves, radio waves, and light waves all show a Doppler shift when they come from a moving object.

Radar (Radio Angle Detection and Ranging), developed and first used in the early years of the Second World War, uses radio waves in the same way as an echo sounder uses sound waves. The radar scanner sends out a beam of radio waves as it rotates and receives the echo bouncing back from any solid object that they reach. Because these radio waves are of very short frequency they behave rather like light (they travel at the speed of light and in straight lines, and so are limited to a range of about 30 miles at sea because they cannot follow the curve of the earth).

The rotating scanner emits the beam and the receiver picks up the returning 'echoes' and transfers them to the cathode ray tube that forms the screen of the radar set. This screen is very similar to a television screen. The electrons print the pattern of the echoes on the inside of the screen, which glows where it is struck by an electron. On a ship's radar screen the ship itself appears as a bright dot in the centre. From this dot a bright arm sweeps round and round. This is the beam of radio waves emitted by the scanner. As the waves bounce back, the shape of the coastline appears and other ships, sailing boats, buoys, show up as bright dots. Since nearly everything will give back an echo, waves near the ship cause 'clutter' on the screen near the centre so that a small yacht is almost invisible. Most radar sets can be set to three scales; a thirty-mile radius for use in the open sea;

a ten-mile radius for the approach to land; and a one-mile radius for harbour or river navigation.

Harbour authorities install radar scanners at important points of a waterway, so that they can control harbour traffic and spot dangerous situations while there is time to warn the ships concerned.

In an aircraft, radar has a far greater range, but is not of value for position finding; however, special sets have been developed to 'scan' clouds to detect storm conditions. By far the most important use of radar is in the ground control of aircraft as they approach airfields for landing.

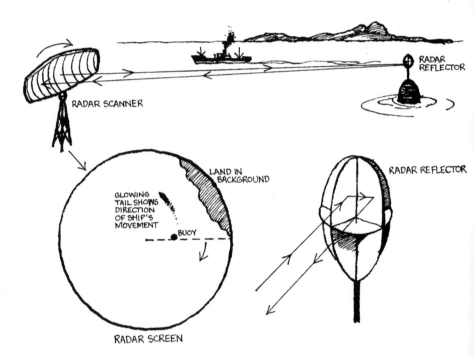

How radar works. The radar scanner rotates, sending out and receiving a continuous stream of radio signals. A radar reflector always sends the signal back along the path it has come. Radar reflectors are used on buoys, yachts and other small craft to ensure that they will be 'seen' on the screen of the approaching vessel. On the radar screen a pencil beam of light picks out reflected objects and they show up as glowing points on the screen as the electrons are concentrated on those parts of the fluorescent tube.

RDF (Radio Direction Finding) equipment can usually be identified by a 'loop' shaped aerial in a prominent position. By rotating the aerial until the radio signal fades out entirely an accurate bearing of the transmitter may be found. Two bearings from different transmitters will give bearings that cross and give a 'fix'.

A more elaborate method is the *Decca* navigational system. This automatic system gives a choice of three bearings from which the navigator can choose the two that cut most nearly at right angles. The Decca system works on the principle that radio waves travel at the speed of light, approximately 186,000 miles per second. If two radio signals are transmitted simultaneously from transmitters at equal distances from the ship, both signals will arrive together. The job of the decometer is to compare the difference in time between the arrival of the two signals. In the Decca system a 'master' station and three 'slave' stations transmit signals at the same instant. A ship at sea chooses the two most convenient 'slaves' and finds the difference in time between the arrival of the master signal and that of the two 'slave' signals. The difference can be plotted along a curved line, a hyperbola, and where the two lines cross that is the ship's position. In practice, the lines are already plotted on the chart in three colours, red, green and purple, representing the three slave stations, and the clock faces are similarly coloured, so that the navigator has only to identify the correct lines to determine his position. Close to land this system is very accurate indeed, and it is possible to arrange that the signals operate a pen that draws out the path of the craft on to a special chart. This system is most widely used in aircraft where a continuous record of the plane's position is more necessary.

Once the craft is more than a hundred miles from the transmitters the accuracy of Decca falls off and a newer system, *Dectra*, is being introduced for trans-Atlantic crossings. A 'master and slave' pair transmit signals from Britain, whilst another pair in Newfoundland send their signals in

A Decca receiver, Courtesy of the Decca Navigator Co. Ltd.

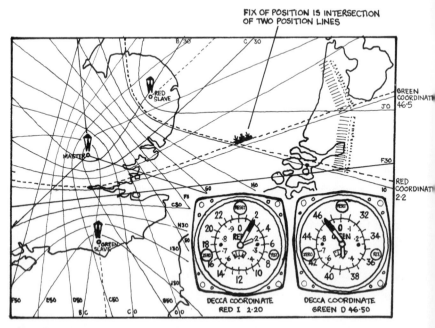

How Decca works.

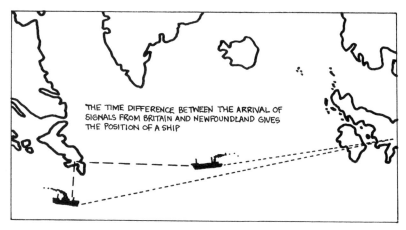

THE TIME DIFFERENCE BETWEEN THE ARRIVAL OF SIGNALS FROM BRITAIN AND NEWFOUNDLAND GIVES THE POSITION OF A SHIP

How Dectra works.

the intervals between the British signals. By comparing the arrival of the two sets of signals the distance from each transmitter can be found. This system is most accurate when the craft is travelling along or almost along the line between the transmitters, and the positions of these have been chosen to cover the usual route taken by most North Atlantic traffic.

You might ask how it is possible to detect a time difference between two radio signals travelling at the speed of light. The measuring equipment makes use of the length of the transmitted waves. Master and slave will each send out a wave of exactly the same length. Each wave is like a sea wave with a crest and a trough and if the ship is an equal distance from each transmitter then the troughs and crests will arrive together. If, however, one transmitter is closer to the ship than the other, then the crests and troughs will arrive independently. By calculating the crest of one wave and the trough of the other the distance from the transmitter may be gauged.

This same principle can be seen in the *Loran* (Long Range Navigation) system. The waves themselves appear on a small screen and by manipulating the dials the two shapes can be made to sit one on top of the other. When this has been completed the figures read from the dials give the amount by which the arrival times of the radio waves differ. By using long waves, as much as one kilometre from crest to crest, these systems are able to cover much greater distances (more than 1,000 miles for the newly-developed Dectra system and 800 miles for Loran) because the long waves follow the curve of the earth.

Measuring very short fractions of a second is possible by lining up the 'waves' of each signal, as in the Loran system. The amount of adjustment needed to bring the two waves together measures the time of difference.

The gyro compass, first introduced in Germany in 1906, is now standard equipment in ocean-going ships. Its prime advantage is that it aligns itself with the earth's axis, giving the direction of 'True North' as opposed to the variable direction of 'Magnetic North', and when set in gimbals maintains its set direction towards the pole in spite of any movement that the ship makes.

The gyroscope, the spinning wheel that is the heart of the gyro compass, is mounted very close to the centre of the ship where wave movement has the least effect. An electric motor rotates the wheel at a very high speed and the wheel takes up its alignment over a period of minutes as the speed builds up. Once it is operating steadily an electric current transfers the heading of the gyroscopes to a series of 'compasses' on or near the bridge where the helmsman is thus able to refer to both magnetic and gyro compasses. Small errors that creep into the gyro heading, known as 'drift', amounting to 1° an hour, are often automatically controlled or are so regular that they can be taken into account when setting the course.

Submarine navigation is only now beginning to come into its own. Jules Verne predicted it all in his book, *Twenty*

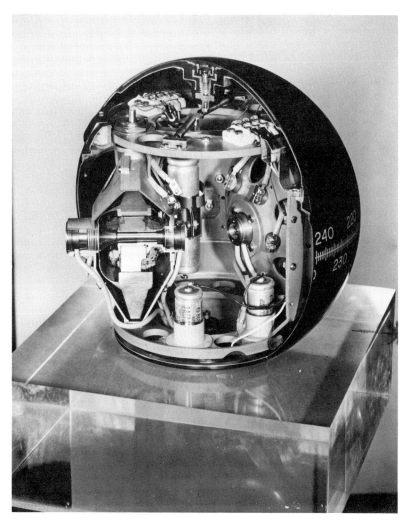

A master gyro. Courtesy of the Decca Navigator Co. Ltd.

Thousand Leagues Under The Sea. In recognition of his gift of a good story the US Navy christened their first atomic-powered submarine *Nautilus* after Captain Nemo's craft. The modern *Nautilus* pioneered a route underneath the polar ice and across the top of the world. There were no charts for her to follow as she dipped beneath the ice near

107

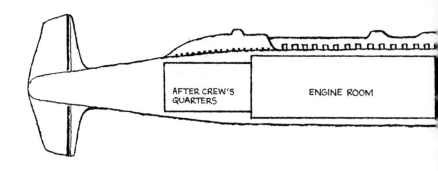

Point Barrow in Alaska. Thirteen echo sounders, bleeping like electronic bats, traced out the walls of a great submarine canyon that was 1,200 feet deep in places and 12 miles wide. Television cameras kept watch overhead to give warning of ice fangs which might project below the general level of the ice. Infrequently, *Nautilus* was able to reach the surface, or to poke a periscope through a hole in the ice and take a star sight in the traditional way to find her position. For the bulk of the time her crew had to rely on their 'inertia' system which is an accurate, electronic 'dead reckoning'. The next time you ride in a car or bus, close your eyes and by the feel of acceleration, turning, slowing down and stopping, try and work out your position as you go along. An 'inertia' system works just like that. A whole battery of gyroscopes are set in motion and every time the submarine alters course or speed, dives or surfaces, the gyroscopes record the movement, however slight. By starting from an exactly calculated position her progress is monitored every second of every day. The movements recorded by the gyroscopes are fed into a computer which is programmed to assemble all the information and produce a position.

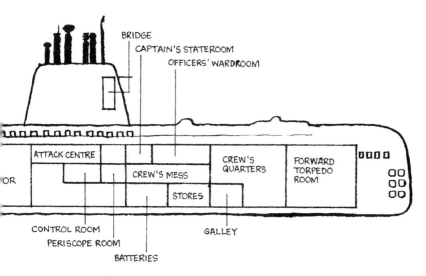

BRIDGE
CAPTAIN'S STATEROOM
OFFICERS' WARDROOM

ATTACK CENTRE

'OR

CREW'S MESS

STORES

CREW'S QUARTERS

FORWARD TORPEDO ROOM

CONTROL ROOM
PERISCOPE ROOM
BATTERIES
GALLEY

United States Submarine *Nautilus.*

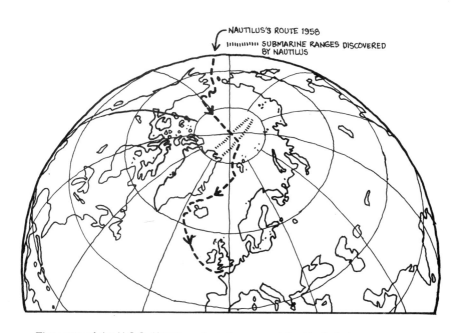

NAUTILUS'S ROUTE 1958
SUBMARINE RANGES DISCOVERED BY NAUTILUS

The route of the U.S.S. *Nautilus* when she crossed the North Pole.

Commander W. R. Anderson, U.S.N., Commanding Officer of the U.S.S. *Nautilus*, on the bridge during a period of low visibility, searches for a spot deep enough to submerge safely under the ice to pass under the North Pole. Courtesy of the Naval Photographic Centre, Naval Station, Washington, D.C., U.S.A.

Submarine navigation will almost certainly be a branch of the art which will receive great attention in the coming years. As we use our mineral resources at an increasing rate, so the search for new sources of energy and raw materials will certainly spread to the sea-bed; already off-shore oil exploration is a major feature in the North Sea. Shipping companies will not be slow to take advantage of the savings in distance, time and money offered by the 'submarine route' to the Pacific. There will be no delays due to fog or bad weather so that the submarine freighters will be able to run to a fixed schedule. But there will have to be great advances in submarine charts—*Nautilus* discovered 9,000-foot mountain ranges that nobody had spotted before.

Lieutenant William Lalor kept his own log of the journey across the North Pole beneath the Arctic ice. He wrote:

'August 2nd 1958. At Lat. 76° 22′ soundings went from 2,000 fathoms to 500 fathoms very abruptly. We were crossing a 9,000-foot submerged mountain range, un-charted and unknown. This feature continued for about

110

Checking the position of U.S.S. *Nautilus* from the inertial navigation system during the final approach to the North Pole.

70 miles when the soundings just as abruptly smoothed out again, about 2,000 fathoms . . .'

When they finally reached the pole on August 3rd they watched:

'. . . in awe [as] our gyro compasses swung, finally to point back where we had been.'

Then the problems of the navigators became really delicate, for there is only one direction at the North Pole—South! But which South? One line of longitude led to Alaska, another to Siberia, both due South.

By August 5th they had reached the Greenland Sea, they hoped:

'In the hours past midnight almost everyone is up waiting for us to clear the ice. The inertial system and our navigator's best plotted position from compasses and distance indicator are only 15 miles apart. The sea water temperature is up to 3°C, indicating we're in the right slot and

111

running into the Gulf Stream branch. Soundings gradually decrease, up to 700 fathoms, indicating we're passing over Nansen's Rise between Greenland and Spitzbergen. Even the ice says we're approaching the edge. Many 400-yard holes, and a lot of one- and two-foot new ice.'

So today's explorers must still use age-old methods of observation in conjunction with modern techniques.

The coming of computers and the launching of satellites is changing the rôle of the navigator. Using new techniques, ships will be able to pinpoint their position to within 300 feet (less than their own length perhaps!). Navigation satellites have been orbiting the earth now for some years, but their use has been restricted to the guidance of the nuclear submarines that are forever nosing their way beneath the oceans.

The basic principle of Satellite Aided Navigation Systems (*Sans*) is very simple. The satellites travel in polar orbits, that is from pole to pole, while the earth rotates beneath them. At a height of 700 miles each satellite completes an orbit in 105 minutes. A tracking system keeps constant watch on the satellites by measuring the Doppler shift. Bearing, height, speed, direction are all fed into a computer, which forecasts the minute by minute position of the satellite for the next twelve hours. This programme is radioed back to the satellite itself. As it circles the earth, it broadcasts its position every two minutes. On the ship's bridge, the navigator can tune the special receiver in to these broadcasts; the receiver will measure the Doppler shift of the satellite during transmission and feed both sets of figures into the ship's computer. Seconds later the print-out gives the navigator his position.

Computers are beginning to take over many tasks on board ship. The Japanese already have plans prepared for ships that are almost completely automatic: tankers and container ships run by a crew of nine computer operators. Few of the latest tankers have a twenty-four hours engine-room crew, computers monitor the engines; the complex

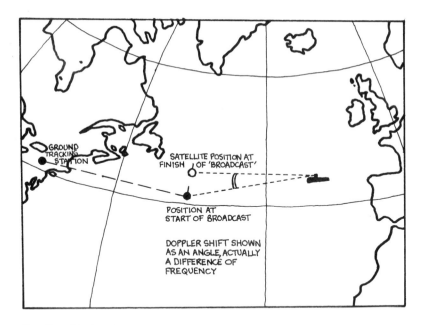

Satellite-aided navigation system (Sans). Because the transit satellite moves so fast, the Doppler shift of its signals can be clearly distinguished and measured to establish the ship's position.

job of loading and unloading the oil, and of opening and closing the valves is automatically controlled and the navigation systems increasingly rely on computer information.

As well as the Sans equipment modern super-tankers are being fitted out with a dead reckoning computer very similar to that used in *Nautilus* where the inertia system is found to be most valuable. Course setting and course alterations to avoid collision and bad weather will also be handled by the computer. We've come a long way from the coracle!

CHAPTER 10

Through the air

Though Leonardo da Vinci (1452–1519) drew plans and sketches for 'flying vehicles' man had to wait until 1783 for his first experience of flight through the air. The first man to do so was named De Rozier and he flew low over the roofs of Paris and was carried for six miles in the 'wrong' direction before he landed. Though he could ascend and descend there was no way of controlling the direction of his flight. By 1852 a small steam engine had been developed which managed to drive Giffard's cigar-shaped balloon at six miles per hour against the wind. This tremendous advance spurred men from many countries to develop bigger,

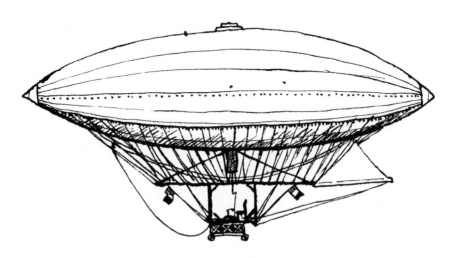

Giffard's balloon.

more rigid balloons and by 1900 these had grown to enormous dimensions so that the term airship was coined to describe the giant launched by Count Zeppelin. These seemingly unwieldy craft were used for bombing raids over Britain during the First World War and as passenger carriers seemed to have a great future in trans-Atlantic travel until the Hindenburg disaster at Lakehurst, New Jersey, in 1937.

It was the First World War that spurred on the development of the heavier-than-air craft and with them was born the need for a new type of chart for use in the tiny cockpit of those early planes. Francis Chichester tells of his first experiment in aerial navigation in his autobiography, *The Lonely Sea and the Sky*.

'The aeroplane was so new that it had not yet been fitted with a compass. I was "flying by Bradshaw" following the railway lines across country, and I wondered if I could fly by the sun. The sky was overcast . . . I climbed up into the cloud and proceeded until I had passed through a 9,000-foot layer of it to emerge at 10,000 feet in brilliant sunshine over a snowy-white field of cloud. Not only had I no compass but no blind-flying instruments at all. I reckoned that if I got into trouble I could force the plane into a spin . . . and that therefore I should be sure to emerge vertically from the cloud. I then wanted to find out how accurately I had carried out this manœuvre, and I used a sound principle of navigation. I fixed my position by the easiest method available—I flew around a railway station low down and read the name off the platform.'

Chichester had more experiences in flying 'blind' and this further passage gives an idea of the problems involved if one has no 'blind flying' instruments.

'I had been flying for seven and three-quarter hours when I reached the south-east coast of Sumatra. The storm clouds were heavier, and there was one big black cloud ahead, but as it was not raining underneath, I held

'I fixed my position by the easiest method available . . .' Francis Chichester, 1929, from his autobiography.

my course. As I got under the middle of the big cloud the bottom seemed to drop out; it was the heaviest rain I had ever known. I whirled round at once to get out, but I was still in the turn in a nearly vertical bank when visibility disappeared, and I was flying blind. As I was already accelerating in the turn, I could not regain a sense of direction or altitude. I sat tight . . . If the speed increased till the struts screamed I eased up the nose. If the acceleration built up sideways I rolled to what I thought was level trim. If that put me upside down I looped . . . Suddenly the sea appeared dead ahead—I was diving straight into it.'

The pilot or navigator of an aircraft has the extra dimension of altitude to cope with and it was soon realised that an instrument basically similar to the aneroid barometer could be used to show the height of the aircraft above sea level. Like the barometer the altimeter measures the weight of the column of air above it; the higher the aircraft flies

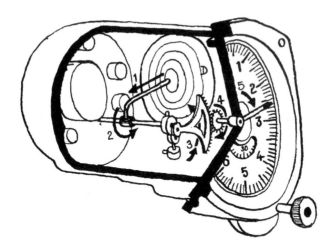

The principal moving parts of an altimeter. As the altitude increases, air pressure decreases. Air escapes through the tube on the right and the diaphragm (D) expands, causing the link to move (1). This causes the rocking shaft to rotate (2). At the end of this shaft is the sector (3), a geared arc with teeth which engages the pinion (4). Because of the ratio between the pinion and the sector, any slight movement of the sector is magnified and indicated by the pointer (5).

the shorter and lighter the column of air. The weight is measured by a delicate capsule that has had most of the air removed, leaving a partial vacuum. As the aeroplane climbs, the air pressure on the capsule lessens and the capsule begins to expand; as the aeroplane descends, the air pressure

Early aeroplanes had simple control panels.

increases, the capsule is compressed and the slight movement is transferred by a simple cog movement to a dial in the cockpit.

Wind, too, has a far greater effect on an aircraft than on a ship. Watch an aircraft flying across wind on a windy day and note its almost crabwise flight. But how does the pilot work out the exact angle that he is being blown off course? Once again the early pilots were forced back to methods of judgement by eye. Francis Chichester again:

'. . . I looked over the side, fixed a point on the water such as a fleck of white, and flew the plane so that this fleck left the side of the fuselage at an angle of, say, five

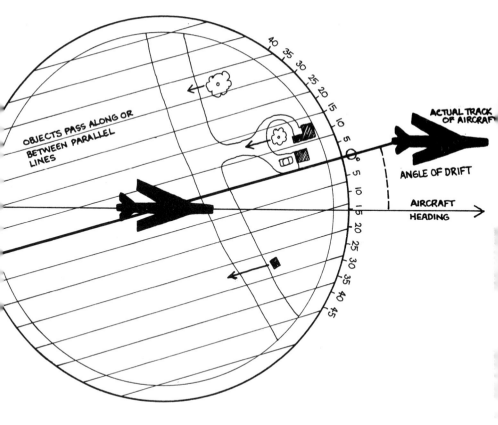

Finding the rate of drift.

degrees. In other words, I made the plane "drift" five degrees as it flew away from that speck. Then I looked back quickly at the compass, and if the reading still showed that the plane was on course, then the five degrees of drift must have been correct . . . I reckoned I could tell the drift to one and a quarter degrees by imagining a five-degree angle split into four.'

By taking three such 'sights' with the plane heading in a different direction each time, Chichester was able to work out the speed and direction of the wind single-handed, something that other early pilots claimed could not be done.

All this happened not so long ago—1931 during the first solo flight from New Zealand to Australia. Later, pilots had bands painted across the wings of their aircraft, angled off to either side. By sighting landmarks and noting the angle of their approach in relation to the painted bands a quick check on drift could be made. Sometimes similar sets of lines are painted along the nose of the aircraft.

A more accurate method of finding the rate of drift was soon developed for commercial aircraft. A vertical sight was built into the bottom of the aircraft and secured firmly along the line of the fuselage. The glass of the sight was engraved with a series of parallel lines and the glass could be rotated within the firmly secured mounting. As the plane passed over a series of landmarks, the glass would be rotated so that the mark travelled between the parallel lines from one side of the sight to the other. When this was done, the amount the glass had been rotated was read from a scale on the mounting and showed the drift.

High-flying jet planes can now be set on a course towards a distant radio beacon. A steady course is maintained for a few minutes, and the bearing of the radio beacon is taken

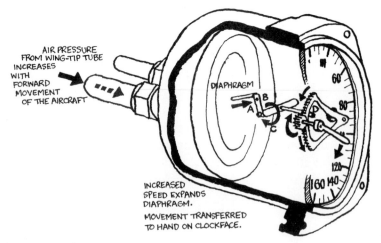

Measuring air speed.

by rotating the aerial so that the radio signal is once more lined up. The amount that the aerial has to be rotated shows how much the plane has been blown 'off course'.

Blind flying is still tricky, but the pilot now has a range of instruments to refer to and the term 'Instrument Flying' is used instead.

Airspeed is measured by comparing the pressure of the air rushing past the wing with the pressure of still air at the altitude at which the plane is flying. Two tiny tubes at one wing-tip in small aircraft or right at the nose of larger jets are all that are needed. One tube is open at the end so that

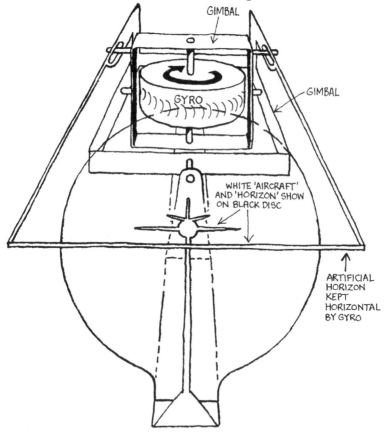

GIMBAL

GIMBAL

GYRO

WHITE 'AIRCRAFT' AND 'HORIZON' SHOW ON BLACK DISC

ARTIFICIAL HORIZON KEPT HORIZONTAL BY GYRO

The pilot can see the 'attitude' of the aeroplane by checking his artificial horizon.

the air is forced inside. The other is closed, but has a ring of tiny pin holes around the sides so that air can get inside. The tubes extend from the wing-tip or nose, right to the cockpit where they are fed into the back of the wind speed gauge. Here the outside air pressure is maintained by the air coming through the tiny pin holes of the closed tube, whilst the air forced through the open-ended tube is fed into a delicate metal capsule very similar to the capsule of the aneroid barometer. As the aircraft gains speed, the pressure increases and the metal capsule expands; this expansion is transferred to a needle and dial by a simple cog system. By watching the air speed indicator the pilot can judge roughly whether or not he is flying a level course. If the nose of the plane is down then his speed will increase; if the plane is climbing then air speed will fall.

A more accurate indicator of the plane's 'attitude' is given by the 'artificial horizon'. A small, heavy gyroscope is mounted so as to remain unmoved whatever movement the plane itself might make. This is done by mounting the gyroscope in a series of gimbals. Held quite steady by the gyro is a fine wire that represents the horizon, whilst mounted in front of it is a small silhouette of a plane. As the control stick is pulled back, the plane begins to rise and so does the small model; but the horizon line held by the gyro remains steady. As the plane banks to turn the small model too dips one wing, but held fast by the spinning wheel the horizon remains level. So the pilot has an automatic check on the 'attitude' of his plane.

A gyroscope is also used to indicate direction in the same way as a magnetic compass and usually the two are mounted together: compass and direction indicator. The small gyroscope will indicate a set direction for a long period and once airborne the pilot takes the magnetic reading from the compass and 'sets' the direction indicator to the same heading. Though the gyro may need re-setting after an hour or more each instrument is a check on the other. Magnetic compass and gyroscope work together.

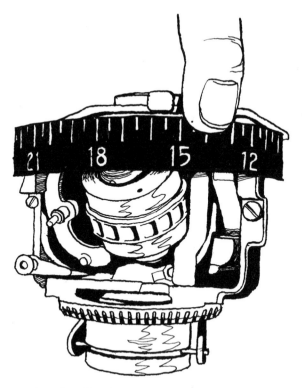

A cutaway section of a directional indicator. The heavy gyroscope is in the centre. The fingernail shaped hollows catch the jet of air to keep the gyroscope spinning.

This is useful as the magnetic compass can behave quite oddly in thunder-storms. On the larger aircraft the magnetic compass automatically corrects the gyro if it starts to wander. Another small gyro set in a vertical axis will show whether the plane has one wing tip higher than the other, though this of course shows up quite clearly in the artificial horizon, whilst any side slip during a turn sets a small agate ball rolling, in a small, curved, liquid-filled tube in the same way that a bubble moves in a spirit level.

Finally, the pilot has to be able to find his position when out of sight of land. This he does in much the same way as the ship's navigator, by observations of the sun, moon and stars. He will however use a different type of sextant

A bubble sextant.

that will provide a 'horizon' even though the plane may be flying above a thick layer of cloud. This instrument is known as a 'bubble sextant'. Instead of using the mirrors to bring the star or sun down to the true horizon, the navigator adjusts the sextant so that sun or star appears to sit in the centre of a small bubble. Though not quite as accurate as the marine sextant the bubble sextant is so quick and easy to use that several sights can be taken, the average giving a position as accurately as the marine sextant would give.

The speed of modern jet planes is now so great that by the time the navigator has worked out the plane's position

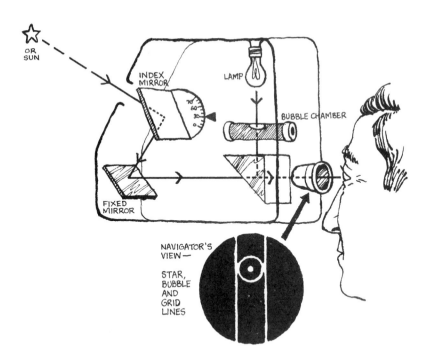

How a bubble sextant works.

it will have travelled fifty miles or more. Hence, to find an instant position a series of radio bearings are used, and these will give a fairly accurate fix in a very short time.

The automatic pilot ('George') will keep a plane flying along a pre-selected course almost indefinitely. The gyros that operate the navigational instruments are 'monitored' by other gyros so that any alteration of the instruments' readings sets up a small electric current sufficient to run a small electric motor. If the aircraft starts to dip the electric current runs the motor connected to the elevators and restores the plane to level flight.

As the approach to land is the most dangerous for ships, so the approach to landing is the most nerve-racking for the pilot, especially if weather conditions are poor. Fog is the great enemy. However, the *Bleu* (Blind Landing Experimental Unit) now enables the pilot to land safely in the

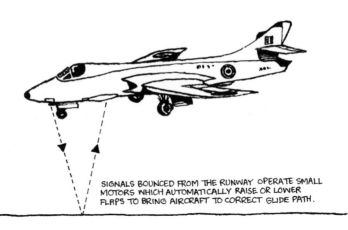

SIGNALS BOUNCED FROM THE RUNWAY OPERATE SMALL MOTORS WHICH AUTOMATICALLY RAISE OR LOWER FLAPS TO BRING AIRCRAFT TO CORRECT GLIDE PATH.

Bleu. Blind landing experimental unit.

thickest of fogs. Radio beams are bounced from the aircraft to the ground and the height of the aircraft above the runway can be measured to within 4 or 5 inches. As the plane glides in, so the radio signals come back more and more rapidly, and these signals can be used to control the electric current that operates the elevators, so that the plane follows the correct curved glide path to the runway. The pilot can, however, take over control if the runway is blocked by some unexpected obstruction.

Computers will soon give ground control a complete picture of all aircraft positions on a global scale. Two satellites, each stationed 22,300 miles above the Equator, could keep a world-wide watch on aircraft and ships almost anywhere in the world. At this great height the satellites appear to hover stationary in the sky.

From a ground station a high frequency signal is beamed to the satellite, which re-broadcasts it over its entire area. This signal, picked up by an aircraft, would vary depending on its angular distance from the satellite. To the information about the course received from the satellite, data regarding the speed and altitude are added and the enlarged signal is beamed back to both satellites. Satellite B now repeats the procedure, which is the drawing of a 'radio position line',

126

and all the information is relayed to the computer at the ground station. As each satellite has produced a position circle the computer works out where these two circles cross and within 60 seconds the pilot has his position.

Ground control also has the position of this and all other aircraft flying under the 'gaze' of the satellites, and the advantages of this are immense. Because at present it is not possible

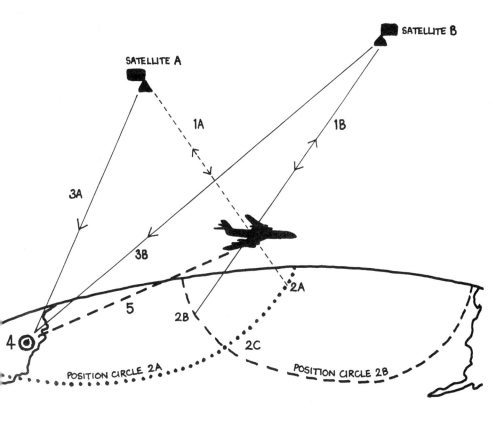

Satellites can keep track of aircraft. Signals (1A and 1B) from the satellite are picked up by the aircraft. Details of the course, speed and altitude are relayed to the satellite, which interprets the signals to form two position circles (2A and 2B). The point at which these cut (2C) is the aircraft's position. This information is relayed back (3A and 3B) to the Ground Control computer (4), which works out the aircraft's latitude and longitude and radios (5) this information to the pilot.

Weather patterns are easily spotted from a satellite. Courtesy of New Zealand Meteorological Services.

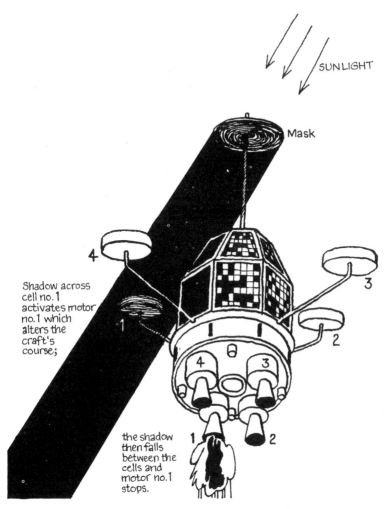

SUNLIGHT

Mask

4

3

Shadow across
cell no. 1
activates motor
no. 1 which
alters the
craft's
course;

1

2

4   3

the shadow
then falls
between the
cells and
motor no. 1
stops.

1   2

A satellite can be kept on course with a system locked on to a star or the sun.

to keep such a close watch on every aircraft, once over the oceans each aircraft is flight planned to be at least 120 miles horizontally from other aircraft flying in the same direction. Those flying in opposite directions are kept at different altitudes, all in the interests of safety. Over land, however, where a much closer check can be kept on each aircraft's position, this 120-mile gap can be reduced to 8 miles. Hence satellite control will make the skies much safer for the greater number of aircraft expected in the future.

The guidance and navigation of satellites and space craft is still in its infancy and yet scientists have developed very complex systems to control and direct unmanned vehicles.

Satellites close to the earth's surface can use the pull of gravity to keep themselves correctly aligned. A heavy weight on the end of a mast provides sufficient control for the present transit satellites. The satellites that orbit thousands of miles from the surface need a system that can work without gravity. One such system is controlled by a series of sensitive light cells. Once in orbit these cells are 'locked' on to the sun or a particular star so that the cells are receiving the full intensity of light. If the satellite drifts off course or out of alignment, then some of the light cells will be blanked off by a suitably positioned shade. The difference between the bright and shaded cells will cause a small electric charge to trigger off guidance rockets that return the satellite to its correct course and position in relation to sun or star.

CHAPTER 11

Mind the rocks!

For the ship's officers, being at sea, miles from land, even in cloudy weather when they cannot fix the ship's position, is a picnic compared with taking their ship through the Straits of Dover on the finest summer day. Now that many ships are so large, navigation close to land and in crowded waters is nerve-racking. The *Nisseki Maru*, a Japanese tanker of 400,000 tons deadweight, takes nearly 23 minutes to stop with her engines full astern all the time. She travels over three miles before coming to a halt. This branch of navigation **and** seamanship is known as pilotage.

The remains of the Roman lighthouse at Dover. Courtesy of R. Warner.

131

The Pharos of Alexandria.

For more than two thousand years now men have built towers to guide their ships safely home. The most famous early lighthouse was the Pharos, built by Sostratus of Cnidus by command of Ptolemy I. Atop its 500-foot tower a brazier guided ships to Alexandria until August 3rd 1303, when an earthquake brought the tower to ruins. So famous was the Pharos that for some centuries Pharos was the word for lighthouse and today the French for searchlight or headlight is phare. The Romans built lighthouses, and remains are still to be seen of the tower that guided the Roman galleys to Dover. Later lights were recorded at St. Catherines, in the Isle of Wight, in 1323, Spurn Head in 1427, and Ilfracombe in 1522. Wreckers would lure ships on to the rocks to gain a valuable cargo by setting up false lights.

Most of the genuine lights were set up and tended by monks until the Dissolution of the Monasteries by Henry VIII. In 1514 Henry granted a charter to a religious group of mariners in Deptford, 'The Guild of Holy Trinity and St. Clement'. So valuable was their work that when the other orders were abolished, this guild was spared. In 1547 they changed their name to 'Trinity House of Deptford Strond', and to this day the Brothers of Trinity House are responsible for the positioning and maintenance of lighthouses, buoys and beacons around the shores of England and Wales. Scottish coasts are the care of the Commissioners for Northern Lights, whilst a similar body operates in Ireland.

Eddystone lighthouse is perhaps the most famous of 'modern' lighthouses. The first Eddystone only stood for five years from 1698 to 1703, when it was destroyed in a violent storm. In 1708 Rudyerd built a wooden tower which lasted until it burned down in 1755. The next tower was of granite and much of the masonry was 'locked' together with dovetail joints. This tower, designed and built by Smeaton, lasted from 1759 until 1881, when the rocks beneath the light-house began to break up! The present Eddystone light was built between 1879 and 1882 by Sir James Douglass, and all the masonry is dovetailed whilst the base is quite solid so that the waves spend their energy before reaching the tower perched on top.

The design of lighthouses as well as lights has changed. The Pharos burnt wood. Later, coal burning lights needing 400 tons of coal a year were introduced. Candles were used until the mid-1800s, when oil-burning lamps became the rule.

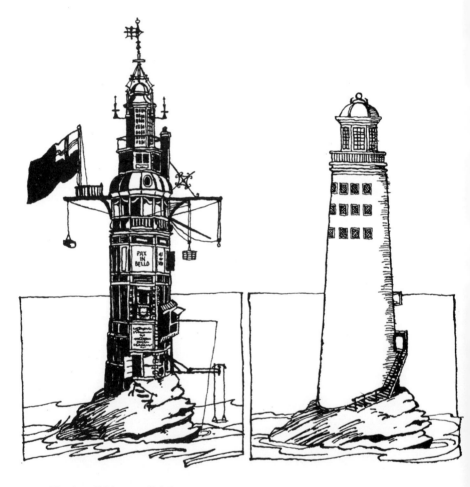

The four Eddystone lighthouses.

Left: 1698 by Henry Winstanley, destroyed by storm in 1703. Right: Rudyerd's wooden tower built 1706–9 but burnt in 1755.

As early as 1763 a reflector that produced a beam of light (parabolic reflector) was used in the Mersey, and with the introduction of the incandescent mantle that transformed the oil to a gas before burning, the power of lights increased tremendously. It was a Frenchman, Augustine Fresnel, who developed a complex lens made up of prisms that concentrated the beam of light to such a degree that it could be seen for twenty or even thirty miles, and though he did this in 1822, Fresnel type lenses are still in use today.

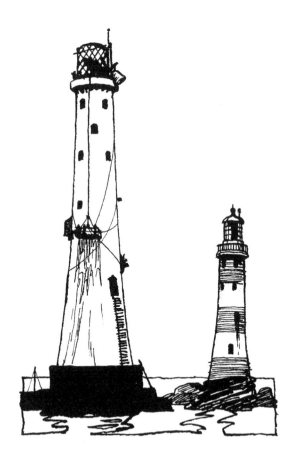

Right: John Smeaton's 1756–59 tower. Left: Sir James Douglass' tower being built in 1882. Electrified 1959–60.

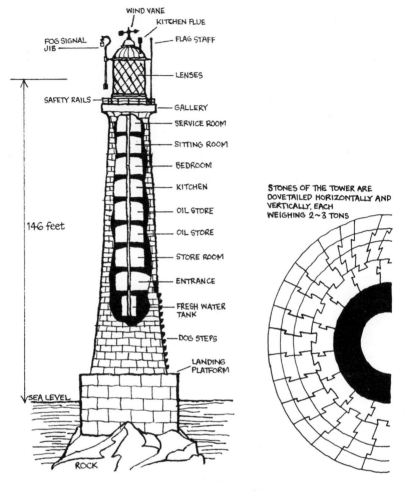

WIND VANE
KITCHEN FLUE
FOG SIGNAL JIB
FLAG STAFF
LENSES
SAFETY RAILS
GALLERY
SERVICE ROOM
SITTING ROOM
BEDROOM
KITCHEN
OIL STORE
146 feet
OIL STORE
STORE ROOM
ENTRANCE
FRESH WATER TANK
DOG STEPS
LANDING PLATFORM
SEA LEVEL
ROCK

STONES OF THE TOWER ARE DOVETAILED HORIZONTALLY AND VERTICALLY, EACH WEIGHING 2~3 TONS

Structure of a lighthouse: the solid masonry of the base resists the storm waves.

For the navigator it is very important that each light can be distinguished easily, and for this purpose each light is given a different 'characteristic'. Longships, the lighthouse off Land's End, has the following characteristic: Occ. W.R. 15 sec. 110 ft. 16 m. This means that the lighthouse shows both a white and red light, the white being visible when the ship is safely clear of danger. If the red light appears then the ship has strayed too close to the land and is in danger of running on to Cape Cornwall or the Runnelstone, off Gwennap Head. The Occ. means that the light is 'occulting', in other words that it is shining for most of the time but goes out for a short interval—the 15 sec. tells us that the long flash and the short period of darkness will together last for fifteen seconds. For a ship steaming up channel the next major light is the Lizard light. This light has a very simple characteristic that couldn't be confused with Longships. The Lizard light is a single white flash every three seconds. Fl. 3 sec. 230 ft. 21 m. The figure of 230 feet gives the height above Mean High Water Springs (the average height of high water during spring tides) and the distance 21 miles is the distance the light is visible in clear weather when viewed from a height of 15 feet above sea level. This height goes back to the days when most navigation was done from the poop of a sailing ship; nowadays the bridge is often nearer 60 feet above sea level. As well as the light at the Lizard two blasts of the siren are sounded at regular intervals during the day or night, when visibility is poor.

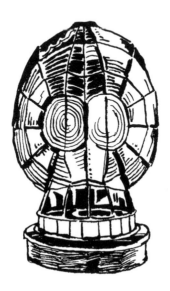

The Fresnel lens.

The Lizard coal fires, 1801.

The higher a lighthouse is the further its light can be seen, so that, where possible, lighthouses are built on cliffs or hills close to the coast. However, not all rocks and shoals are situated conveniently near to cliffs, and so the light may be far out to sea.

Where it is not possible to station a lighthouse, a lightship may be moored to mark dangers. The Goodwin Sands, grave-yard of hundreds of ships, is marked by two lightships, for the shifting sands offer no foundation for a lighthouse. The new Nantucket lightship marks the seaward end of the dreaded Nantucket shoals which the Admiralty Pilots describe:

'These shoals extend forty miles south-east of Sankaty Head lighthouse, and render this one of the most dangerous parts of the United States coast'.

In 1620 the *Mayflower* narrowly avoided these shoals, altered course to pass to the north of them and so altered history, landing at Plymouth Rock, New England, instead of in New Jersey as they had intended. The new Nantucket lightship is the world's most isolated lightship, being moored ⊾1 miles from land.

Modern lighthouses still perform the same job as their ancestors, but much more efficiently. The new Dungeness light is the third built there, because the shingle beach is

Lizard point today. Courtesy of Aerofilms Ltd.

being extended all the time by wave action. This has left the first light a mile inland. The new light is slimmer, yet stronger, being built of pre-stressed concrete rings. Once the full tower of rings had been erected, the wire cables were hauled incredibly tight so that the rings became one solid mass.

The record for the highest lighthouse certainly goes to Japan, where the light itself is perched at the top of a 456-foot radio mast. Japan also leads the field in providing a new source of power for lighthouses—an experimental light in the Sea of Japan is run on electricity produced by solar batteries which recharge themselves during the hours of sunlight.

The light from a lighthouse must be powerful enough to be seen in conditions of poor visibility, though a blanket of fog will make it quite invisible, and yet in times of good

The *Nantucket* lightship, off station for refitting. Official U.S. Coast Guard photograph.

The new Dungeness light. Courtesy of Keystone Press Agency Ltd.

visibility a much less powerful one would be quite sufficient and much more economic to operate. To make this possible some lighthouses in the United States have been equipped with two complete lights. The less powerful is 1,400,000 candelas (approximately the equivalent of $1\frac{1}{2}$ million candles). Four miles away a small monitor light is set up. If visibility becomes so bad that the monitor light cannot be seen then automatically the more powerful (14m. candelas) light is brought into action.

Not every headland has a lighthouse perched on top of it; more often the off-lying dangers are marked with a buoy. For ships bound for further ports the lighthouses are quite close enough for one to come into sight before the last one dips below the horizon, so buoys mark the local danger points for vessels navigating close inshore in that particular area. Each buoy has its own characteristic light and conforms in shape and colour to the system of buoyage used locally. There are two basic systems in use throughout the world:

The Shakkuri light beacon in the Sea of Japan, powered by solar batteries. Courtesy of the Japanese Ministry of Transport.

1 The Lateral System, used in Britain, USA, Canada, Australia, New Zealand and the Far East. In this system the buoys mark out a 'safe' channel.

2 The Cardinal System, used on the French coast and in most European waters. This system marks the 'dangers' and the shape and colour of the buoys tells the navigator which side to leave each buoy.

In using the lateral system the navigator must know the direction of the main stream of the flood (incoming) tide. When sailing with the flood tide the port side of the channel is marked with red or red and white 'can'-shaped buoys, whilst the starboard side of the channel is marked with black or black and white conical buoys. Each buoy is numbered, starting with No. 1 at the seaward end of the channel. Some of the buoys are lighted at night. The port hand buoys show a red flashing light giving up to 4 flashes, or a white light giving 2 or 4 flashes. The starboard hand

The lateral system of buoyage.

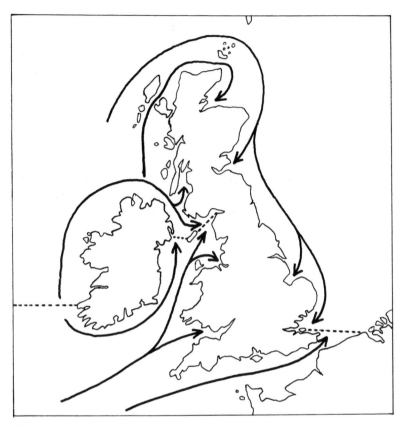

The main streams of the flood tides.

buoys give either 1 or 3 white flashes. If there is a sandbank or other obstruction in the middle of the channel, then it will be marked with spherical buoys. These have black and white horizontal stripes where the main channel is to the left and red and white stripes where the main channel is to the right. A green buoy with a green flashing light always indicates a wreck. The main difficulty with the lateral system is that when going against the main stream of the flood tide all the buoys, their colours, shapes and lights must be read in reverse. The greatest advantage is that the channel, however narrow and winding, is clearly marked out on either side.

The Cardinal system is mostly used along coastlines where the dangers are isolated and may be well off-shore. The area around a patch of rocks or a wreck is divided into four equal quadrants, N., E., S. and W. The shape and colour of the buoy tells the navigator which side is the safe side to pass. Again, the basic colours are black, white and red, and green still indicates a wreck. Though the United States uses the lateral system and so marks out a 'safe' channel, the starboard side of the channel is marked with red buoys and the port with black.

Pilotage, then, is the navigation of the vessel in coastal waters, making constant use of the wide variety of lights, buoys and marks to keep a constant check on the ship's position.

The simplest way to 'fix' the ship is to take two compass bearings of prominent features that are clearly marked on the chart. On a small ship or yacht this is most easily done

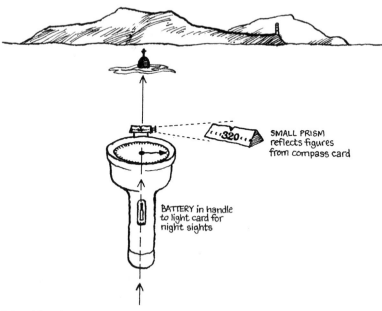

SMALL PRISM reflects figures from compass card

BATTERY in handle to light card for night sights

A hand bearing compass.

with a hand-bearing compass. The compass is held up to the eye and the navigator looks along the small sights at the lighthouse, headland or buoy, and at the far edge of the compass a small prism reflects the reading of the compass card so that it appears immediately below the 'target'. This

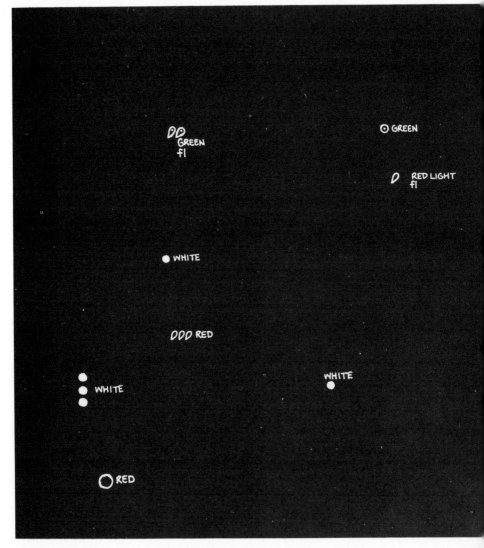

The officer on the bridge must know what all these lights mean.

reading must now be corrected for magnetic variation, that is the difference between True North and Magnetic North. This can be found by referring to the chart, finding the nearest compass rose on which will be printed the variation, the year this figure was established and the amount that

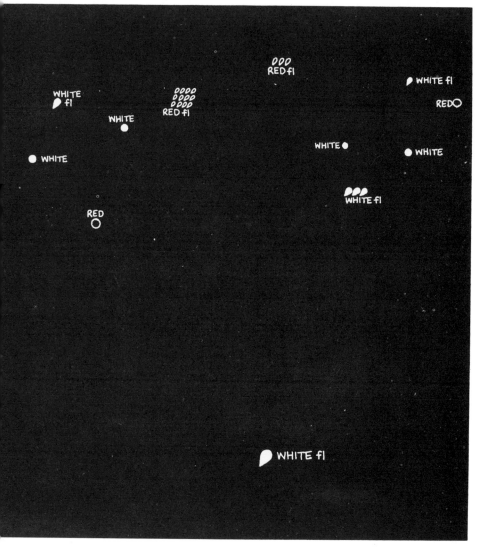

the variation alters from year to year. As well as the allowance for variation, an allowance for deviation must be made. Deviation is the amount the compass needle is displaced by the steel and electrical equipment on the ship itself. This is found from a small table that gives the amount of deviation

GREEN flash

WREC

GREEN LIGHT

RED fl

WHITE LIGHT

RED fl

WHITE LIGHT

WHITE LIGHT

WHITE LIGHT

WHITE LIGHT

RED LIGHT

The night scene on pages 146 and 147 would look like this in daylight.

for each particular heading. If you consider the amount of steel in a modern ship, and the length of time she must remain on the building ways being hammered and battered, it is not surprising that the entire ship becomes one large magnet. Where possible the building ways are aligned north

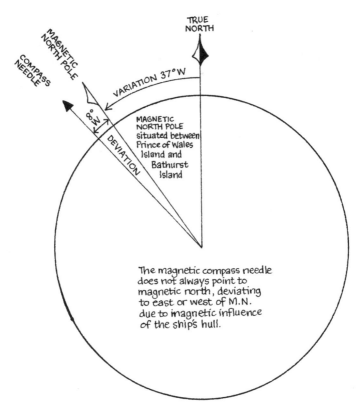

Deviation — what is it?

and south so that the effect of deviation will be less. The amount of deviation is found by 'swinging the ship', so that a pair of landmarks are kept in line on a known magnetic bearing. For each 10° a compass bearing is taken of the two landmarks and the amount by which this bearing differs from the correct magnetic bearing is the deviation. The important fact to remember in a small boat is 'never to leave any steel object near the steering compass'; a jack-knife in your pocket may put you 6–8° off course if you sit close to the compass and you may end up on a sand-bank or, even worse, on the rocks.

Deviation is kept to a minimum in larger ships by placing a series of small compensating magnets at different distances

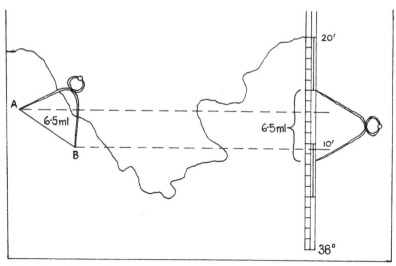

Measuring distance from the latitude scale.

from the compass itself. This is a skilled task and should only be done by qualified compass adjusters.

Now that we are aware of the various corrections that must be applied to every compass bearing that we take, let's look at other ways of fixing the ship's position.

The most necessary piece of equipment is a correct chart of the area. The widest range of charts is published by the Admiralty. They are published in a variety of scales.

Ocean charts: very small scale covering a wide area.

Coastal charts: larger scale for navigating close to land.

Plan charts: largest scale, full details of harbours.

Most Admiralty charts are drawn on the Mercator projection, which enables the navigator to draw a straight line from A to B to represent his course. On these charts lines of latitude are not evenly spaced; the gap between them widens as the poles are approached. Lines of longitude appear as straight lines parallel to one another. Distance is measured along the latitude scale at either side of the chart

151

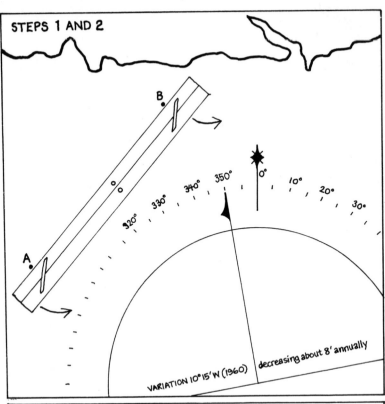

STEPS 1 AND 2

B

320° 330° 340° 350° 0° 10° 20° 30°

A

VARIATION 10°15'W (1960)   decreasing about 8' annually

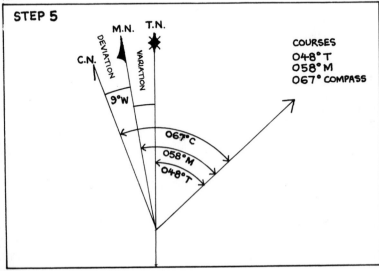

STEP 5

C.N.   M.N.   T.N.

DEVIATION   VARIATION

9°W

COURSES
048° T
058° M
067° COMPASS

067°C
058°M
048°T

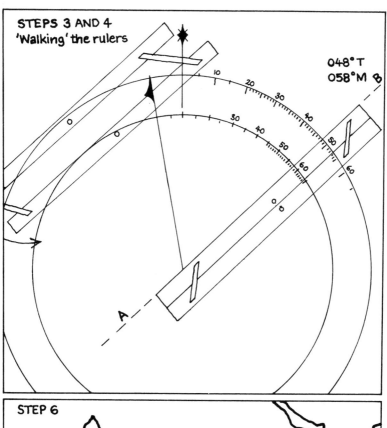

STEPS 3 AND 4
'Walking' the rulers

048° T
058° M B

10
20
30
40
50
60

30
40
50
60

A

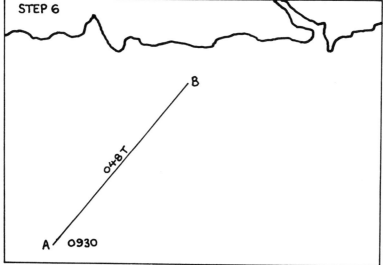

STEP 6

B

048 T

A 0930

Laying off a course.

153

(*never* along the longitude scale at top and bottom of the chart). 1 minute of latitude equals 1 nautical mile. As the parallels of latitude are spaced further apart nearer the poles *it is important that the navigator use that part of the scale that is level with the distance being measured on the chart.*

Here is a step-by-step method for laying off a course. The first task is to lay off on the chart the course which you wish to follow. To do this you will need a pair of parallel rulers or a Douglas protractor.

Step 1 Mark on the chart points A and B.

Step 2 Place one edge of the parallel rulers along A–B.

Step 3 'Walk' the rulers, making sure they stay parallel to A–B, to the centre of the nearest compass rose.

Step 4 Read off the 'True' course from the outside ring and the 'Magnetic' course from the inside ring. If the chart is up-to-date, there will be no need to allow for the small amount of shift in variation that occurs in two or three years.

Step 5 Draw up the small compass diagram. Put in T.N., M.N. and then from the deviation table put in COM-PASS NORTH. From the diagram the compass course to be steered will be obvious.

Step 6 Mark your starting position A with your time of departure and your course with the compass heading.

Once under way the navigator must take every opportunity to 'fix' the position of the ship. This is done by a variety of bearings, one of which has already been described. The way in which the navigator plots his position from the bearings is the reverse of the method used to lay off a course.

Step 1 Find the 'True' bearing of the lighthouse or buoy by drawing the small compass diagram.

Step 2 Place the parallel rulers across the centre of the nearest compass rose so that the edge lies along the 'True' bearing figure.

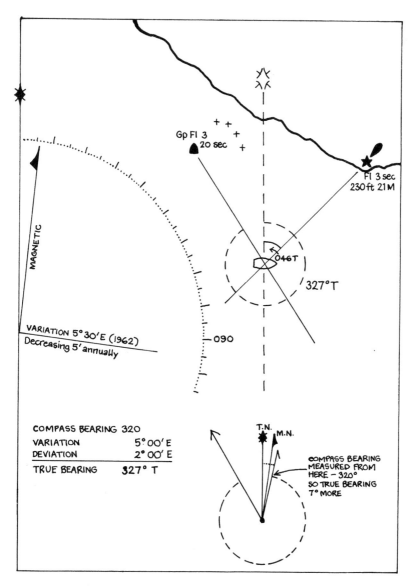

A simple two-bearing fix.

Step 3 'Walk' the rulers across the chart until the edge passes through the chart symbol of the lighthouse or buoy.

Step 4 Lightly draw in the bearing.

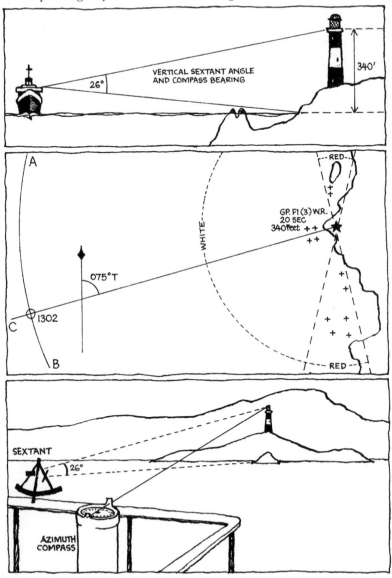

Compass bearing and vertical sextant angle.

Step 5 Repeat the process for the second bearing.

Step 6 Where the two bearings cross draw a small circle. Write in the time of the 'fix' and the log reading preceded by a small triangle.

To mark off a distance along a bearing the dividers are set to the required distance by using the latitude scale. This distance is then stepped off along the bearing.

Once you have mastered the technique of laying off a course and bearing there are four simple ways of 'fixing' the ship's position, by compass bearings and sextant angles.

1 *Simple transit and vertical sextant angle.* In the case where a beacon and a lighthouse are in line (in transit), the navigator measures the angle between the top of the tower and the sea level at its base. Using his tables he can then find out how far he is from the lighthouse and the transit gives him his bearing.

2 *Compass bearing and vertical sextant angle.* If there is no convenient beacon in line with the tower or lighthouse, then at the same time as the sextant angle is taken a compass bearing is taken as well, then again the 'distance off' and the bearing will fix the ship's position.

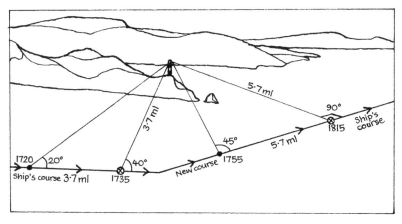

Four point bearing and doubling the angle on the bow.

3 *The 'four point' bearing.* This is a useful method of fixing the ship's position if there is only one prominent feature in view. First note the ship's course and then plot the point where the lighthouse appears 45° on the bow. Note carefully at this point the reading on the ship's log to see how far the ship travels between this bearing and the next. Then watch the lighthouse and note the point when it appears directly abeam, that is at 90° to the ship's course. Take the reading of the ship's log and find out how far the ship has travelled between the two bearings. This distance will be the same as the distance of the ship from the lighthouse at the last bearing. If, however, you wish to alter course before the lighthouse is abeam, it is only necessary to take a bearing at any angle smaller than 45° and then plot the position when the angle has doubled. This method is useful at night, when it is not possible to take a vertical sextant angle because it is not possible to see the sea at the base of the lighthouse.

The disadvantage of the 'doubling the angle' methods is that you have to take the bearings at a particular time, and it is important that a straight course be kept in between the two bearings. Neither of these two may be possible, so another method must be used in which any two bearings of the one object can be used to give the ship's position. This method is known as the 'running fix'.

4 *The Running Fix.* A bearing of the lighthouse is taken when convenient, and a reading of the ship's log is noted at the same time. A careful note of the ship's course is kept even though the ship may have to alter course before the next bearing is taken. The ship steams on until the new bearing is nearly at 90° to the first bearing, then a second bearing of the lighthouse is taken. The navigator then lays off his bearings on the chart. There are three stages in working out position by a running fix.

Step 1 Lay off the first bearing.

Step 2 From anywhere along that bearing, lay the course and distance sailed between the bearings. From the point that represents the 'end' of the distance steamed, lay off a line parallel to the first bearing. This is the transferred position line.

Step 3 Lay off the second bearing. The point at which the second bearing crosses the transferred position line is

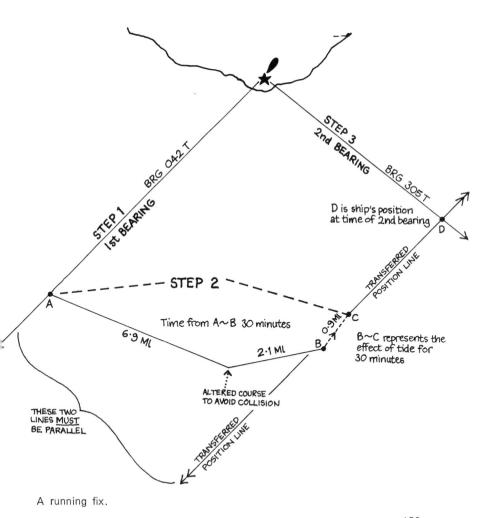

A running fix.

the actual position of the ship at the time of the second bearing.

In coastal waters the navigator must take the tides into account every hour of his watch. But what makes tides? The answer is simple—the pull exerted by the gravity of the moon and to a smaller extent the sun. If there were no land masses in the way the tide would sweep around the earth in two huge crests separated by two low water troughs. However, the gravitational pull of the moon leaves the water as the moon crosses the continents. The water is released and swings back towards the other end of the ocean just as water in the bath will swing from end to end when pushed regularly. As the high crest of the tide reaches coastal inlets the movement changes from a vertical one to a tidal stream. If the inlet has a wide mouth and then becomes rapidly much narrower, like the Bristol Channel, then the water is forced to rise to a great height. At the mouth of the Channel off Lundy Island the rise is 23 feet. By the time the tide reaches Cardiff on the northern shore it has been raised to 37 feet, and eventually reaches 42 feet at Avonmouth.

As the shorelines converge, and the tide has to fight against the outflowing water from the Severn, it is slowed down quite considerably, but it still has to reach its high water mark and so rises several feet instantaneously, forming the famous Severn Bore, a wave four or five feet high that moves upstream from Sharpness Docks moving at about four knots. Where the river narrows, however, its speed increases to about 12 knots at Rosemary. Though the Bristol Channel tides are exceptional the navigator must always bear these things in mind. Most of his information will be contained on the chart itself in a series of little arrows that indicate the speed and direction of the tide, or in a small table that gives the direction of the tide for every hour. This is most valuable when the tide moves in many directions over the twelve-hour period instead of simply 'in and out', so that extra care and vigilance are required.

The Severn Bore. Courtesy of Barnaby's Picture Library.

For the navigator tides pose several problems.

1. A following tide causes the ship to travel further than the log shows.

2. A foul tide slows the vessel down but makes the log run faster.

3. A cross tide puts the ship off course to one side or the other.

4. A tide that is flowing at an angle either on the bow or stern sets the ship to one side of her intended course and either slows her down or increases her speed.

For the first two there is little that the navigator can do, except to allow for the difference between speed through the water, as measured by the log, and the actual speed over the ground. For cross tides, either at right angles to the course or at an angle the navigator can either work out where the tide has set him over the last hour or so, or he

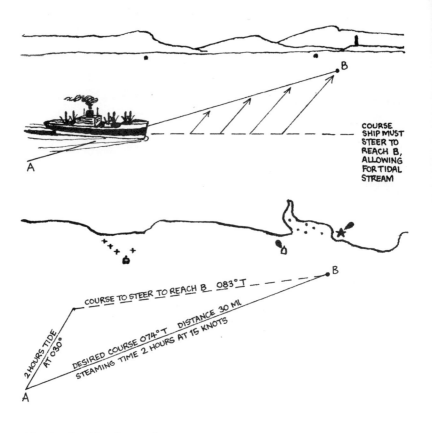

COURSE SHIP MUST STEER TO REACH B, ALLOWING FOR TIDAL STREAM

B

A

B

COURSE TO STEER TO REACH B 083° T

DESIRED COURSE 074° T DISTANCE 30 MI.

STEAMING TIME 2 HOURS AT 15 KNOTS

2 HOURS TIDE AT 030°

A

Allowing for tide when setting a course.

can steer a course that will counteract the force of the tidal stream. This is quite a simple procedure.

Step 1 Lay off your course from A to B. Measure the distance to be sailed and work out how long this leg of the voyage will take.

Step 2 From the tide figures for the area, work out the strength and direction of the tide for the period above.

Step 3 From A, lay off the direction and run of the tide. This establishes point C.

Step 4 From C, lay off the course that will take you to B.

Not enough and then too much: the tide under the Thames bridges.

Although tides cause some navigational problems, without them many great ports of the world would be idle backwaters. The tide that sweeps the colliers up the Thames has to be taken at the right time. At low tide there is only six feet of water by Westminster Bridge, but at high tide there will be so much that the larger ships cannot clear the low slung curve of Hammersmith suspension bridge; so it is most important that the ship's navigator be able to predict the height of the tide for any time of the day or night. As well as this, he must take into account whether or not he is fully loaded, and lastly he can't afford to dawdle for there are eighteen bridges to clear between Tower Bridge and Wandsworth.

Some ports have grown to importance because the tides they experience have a different characteristic to them. Southampton is noted for its 'double high water', which gives the large liners a longer period than usual of deep water in which to manœuvre. There have been many attempts to explain why the tide at Southampton should behave in such an irregular manner and, although no one explanation is completely satisfactory, the theory that the second 'high' arrives from Spithead, along the NE coast of the Isle of Wight, seems to be the most likely. Whatever

Southampton Docks. Courtesy of Aerofilms Ltd.

the reason, Southampton has prospered because of it, as has Le Havre on the French side of the Channel, which has the same long period of high water.

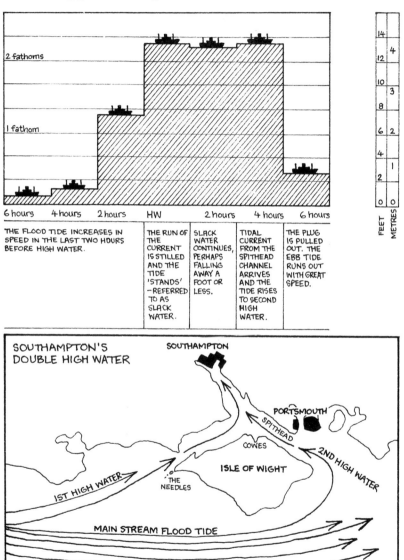

THE FLOOD TIDE INCREASES IN SPEED IN THE LAST TWO HOURS BEFORE HIGH WATER.	THE RUN OF THE CURRENT IS STILLED AND THE TIDE 'STANDS' – REFERRED TO AS SLACK WATER.	SLACK WATER CONTINUES, PERHAPS FALLING AWAY A FOOT OR LESS.	TIDAL CURRENT FROM THE SPITHEAD CHANNEL ARRIVES AND THE TIDE RISES TO SECOND HIGH WATER.	THE PLUG IS PULLED OUT. THE EBB TIDE RUNS OUT WITH GREAT SPEED.

Tides made Southampton a great port.

Errors in navigation have led to many disasters at sea. Sometimes, however, the error lies in the charts and instruments that the navigator must use. Sometimes the cause is bad seamanship.

On November 5th 1902, the steamer *Elingamite* sailed from Sydney, bound for Auckland. Four days later when rounding the northern tip of New Zealand she struck West King, one of the Three King islands and sank within twenty minutes. Altogether 46 people lost their lives.

The channel between the Three Kings and Cape Maria Van Diemen is fifteen miles wide and Captain Attwood estimated that he was six or seven miles south of the jagged rocks. But his estimation proved incorrect—why?

First, he didn't know how far the *Elingamite* had sailed in the previous twenty-four hours as the log had broken; though his estimate of the speed was fairly accurate, it was not accurate enough. Secondly, the currents as marked on the chart could sometimes run equally strongly in the opposite direction.

Added to these two unknowns was fog, but in spite of this the *Elingamite* did not slacken speed until half-an-hour before the wreck. Had soundings been taken then any depth of less than 100 fathoms (600 feet, 200 metres) would have indicated danger. Soundings were due to start at 11 a.m. but the ship struck at 10.45 a.m.

Captain Attwood's certificate was suspended for a year and he was ordered to pay £50 costs. His career was finished and he found employment as a tally clerk with a coal company.

Nine years later HMS *Cambrian* reported that the Three Kings were incorrectly charted. A survey ship, the *Terra Nova*, was sent and the position of the rocks was found to be $1\frac{1}{4}$ miles further south than was marked on the chart. The inquiry was re-opened. Other witnesses were called who vouched for the fact that the currents could flow in a variety of directions, and that the speed of the vessel was as Captain Attwood had estimated. As a result Captain Attwood was

The *Elingamite* wreck. Who was to blame? Photo: Courtesy of the *Auckland Star*, New Zealand.

cleared of blame. The final puzzle as to why the engines didn't go full astern when the rocks were sighted was not solved until sixty-six years later, in 1968. As the *Elingamite* had run in towards the rocks, her propeller had passed over another reef on which it jammed as it began to go astern, but it took divers many weeks to find the buckled propeller blades to prove this point.

The loss of the *Andrea Doria* in 1956 could perhaps be called a 'radar aided' collision. The disaster occurred some eight or nine miles from the Nantucket lightship, an area where fog is frequent.

The *Andrea Doria*, 29,083 tons, was the new flagship of the Italia Line and had sailed from Genoa bound for New York. The vessel that sank her, the *Stockholm*, was less than half her size, but, built in Sweden with the chance of sailing through ice, her bows had been strengthened.

On the night of July 26th 1956 the two vessels approached one another and on each bridge the radar set warned of the approach of the other.

The *Andrea Doria*. Courtesy of the Press Association Ltd., London.

The *Andrea Doria* was in fog, she had slowed her speed by just one knot to 22 knots, while her siren boomed out the regulation long blast of warning every minute. She went ahead on her course.

The *Stockholm* was not in fog, her speed was 18 knots, and the officer of the watch noted the *Andrea Doria* on the radar screen when she was twelve miles off. With the combined speeds of the two vessels this distance was covered in 18 minutes.

Each officer anxiously watched the approach of the other ship. The navigator on the *Andrea Doria* did not want to alter course to starboard as this would take him toward the shoal water to the north of the Nantucket lightship. He watched the *Stockholm* on the radar screen and, though she was almost dead ahead, he had no doubt she would pass on the starboard side of the *Andrea Doria*. This meant he could alter course to port, away from the shallow water.

But the collision rules state:

'When two power-driven vessels are meeting end on or nearly end on, so as to involve risk of collision, each shall alter her course to *starboard*, so that each may pass on the port side of the other.'

On the *Stockholm* the officer watched the approaching dot on the radar screen, but because of the intervening fog he could not see the vessel herself nor her lights which would give him an idea of her heading. Suddenly the look-outs reported 'lights to port', so quite correctly the *Stockholm* altered course to starboard.

On the *Andrea Doria* the *Stockholm* was expected to pass on the starboard side. Because of the fog they could not see her nor her lights. When they did see her the *Stockholm* had already altered course and seemed to be crossing their bows. 'Tutto sinistra', hard-a-port! But it was the wrong way. With her greater speed the *Andrea Doria* surged across the reinforced bows of the *Stockholm*, which cut deep into the liner's side, from her upperworks to the emptied fuel tanks below the waterline. She quickly heeled to a great angle, which prevented many of the lifeboats from being launched, and after 11 hours she foundered. Fortunately several ships were nearby so that 1,663 of the 1,706 on board were saved.

Why didn't the radar set prevent this disaster? Bearings taken from a radar screen are 99.5 per cent accurate! But that 0.5 per cent represents nearly 2°; 2° on a small protractor may seem very little, but extend those 2° from the pole to the Equator and that tiny distance has grown to 120 miles! In the same way the bearings of ships when seen on the small screen of the radar set are reduced so much that they can become almost invisible, but none the less fatal. Confident that the radar screen would prevent collisions the captain of the *Andrea Doria* sailed at almost full speed through fog and at that speed altering course to starboard as the regulations demanded meant that he would be heading towards the dangerous Nantucket shoals. So, against regulations, he altered course to port.

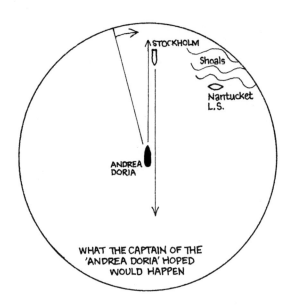

WHAT THE CAPTAIN OF THE
'ANDREA DORIA' HOPED
WOULD HAPPEN

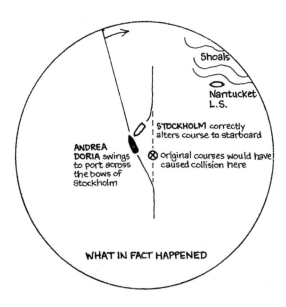

STOCKHOLM correctly
alters course to starboard

ANDREA
DORIA swings
to port across
the bows of
Stockholm

Original courses would have
caused collision here

WHAT IN FACT HAPPENED

Why the *Andrea Doria* and the *Stockholm* were in collision.

One great disadvantage of the standard radar set is that the movement of the vessel itself is not shown. The ship is the stationary central point on the screen and everything else appears to move, even the land. So though the radar set gives a true picture of the positions of vessels and nearby land, the true movement of the vessels is quite distorted. True motion radar, introduced in 1956, does away with this distortion.

A recent disaster that came about through bad pilotage was the wreck of the *Torrey Canyon*. On a voyage from the Persian Gulf via the Cape of Good Hope, the 118,285-ton (deadweight) tanker had almost reached her destination, Milford Haven. The agents had urged speed to take advantage of coming spring tides necessary to berth the heavily loaded tanker. Her course should have taken her to the west of the Scilly Isles but wind and currents set her up-channel

The loss of the *Torrey Canyon*. Courtesy of Barnaby's Picture Library, London.

by several miles. To save half-an-hour the captain decided to take his huge ship between the Scillies and the Seven Stones, a group of rocks awash at low tide, so checking the ship's position both by radar and cross bearings the captain conned the tanker into the narrow passage.

Much of the hard work and concentration has been taken out of steering an accurate course by the use of an 'automatic pilot' which keeps the ship's head on a pre-set course by means of gyroscopes connected to the steering mechanism, though alterations of up to $3°$ can be made by hand. Without switching off the automatic pilot the captain eased the bow of the tanker around to port. Before his ship was fully round on her new course the captain saw that the channel was partially blocked by fishing vessels with their nets out. A quick decision by the captain and the helmsman threw the wheel over to starboard, the automatic pilot was switched off for the turn and then switched on again. But a radar fix and cross bearings showed that the Seven Stones were too close to port for comfort. 'Tutto sinistra', hard-a-port! the captain shouted as he decided to risk the narrow passage in spite of the fishing boats. The helmsman swung the wheel hard over and nothing happened. The tanker ploughed on towards the rocks. The helmsman called to the captain on the wing of the bridge; precious seconds slipped by before the captain realised that the automatic pilot was switched on. But by then it was too late; seconds later the huge tanker ripped out her bottom plates on the western edge of Pollard Rock.

The rest of the story is the massive cleaning-up operation to deal with the 100,000 tons and more of crude oil that spilled into the sea.

CHAPTER 12

How do animals and birds navigate?

The short answer to this question is, 'We don't really know'. Many people have tried to find out and there have been dozens of theories, but we still don't know.

Early man soon noticed that during the winter some birds disappeared and reappeared the following spring. Swallows gathered in reed beds before disappearing, so it was believed that they hibernated in the mud beneath the reeds! Cuckoos were supposed to change into hawks! In time beliefs changed; the swallows were seen to fly off over the horizon, bound for the moon, said the Bishop of Hereford!

Nowadays we know that certain breeds of birds and animals, insects and fish migrate, following a seasonal pattern perhaps, or in the search for food. Greylag geese from Siberia fly across the Himalayas to escape the Siberian

Bound for the moon!

winter. The swallows from England and France winter in South Africa, whilst the longest journey of all is made by the Arctic terns that fly from the Canadian Arctic down the full length of the Atlantic Ocean to the Antarctic.

How do they know the way? The best clue seems to come from the work of a German researcher, Dr. Kramer. He suspected that birds navigated by noting the position of the sun in the sky, so he constructed a special cage fitted with windows and mirrors. Under this he was able to lie and note the direction of flight when the bird saw the sun. When the

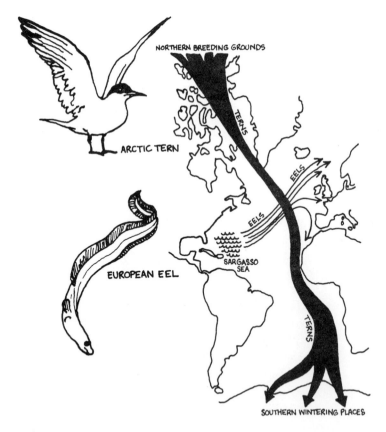

Terns travel almost from pole to pole, whilst the tiny eel reaches the rivers of Europe from the Sargasso Sea.

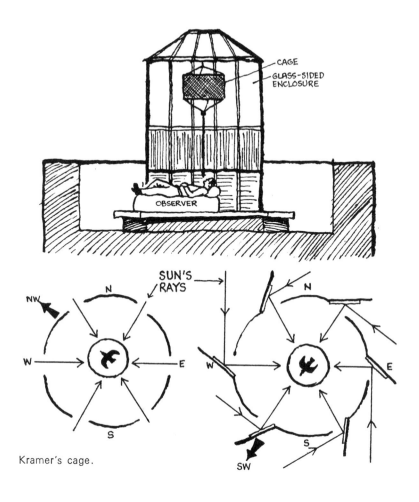

Kramer's cage.

sun came through the windows the birds flew to the north-west. When the mirrors reflected the sun and altered its apparent position by 90°, then the birds flew to the south-west—90° from their first flight. Supporting this idea was the fact that, although birds travel after dark on clear nights, they do not travel in fog or in bad weather. Homing pigeons were a puzzle to Dr. Matthews. How could they find their own loft from a whole variety of distant points after they had travelled in a closed box in a railway wagon? On

175

release the pigeon circled for a few seconds and then took up the correct course for home. Dr. Matthews suggested that the pigeon knew the position of the sun in the sky at his own loft for any hour of the day. In a few seconds' circling he compared the position of the sun with what it ought to be if he was near home. If the sun was lower in the sky, then he must fly south to bring it higher. But this meant that the pigeon must be able to 'tell the time' very precisely and to be able to judge angles even more precisely. That they can 'tell the time' has been shown by altering the length of their days and nights with lights. If this was continued for some time, then they lost their fine homing ability. Once the pigeon was on his correct course for home, he would be able to pick out the loft from familiar landmarks as he neared home.

Birds migrate at night providing the weather is clear. They tend to fly towards a bright moon, and the fact that thousands dash themselves to pieces against lighthouses suggests that it is the moon and stars from which they take their direction.

Migrating fish and eels still pose many unanswered problems, the eels being the most puzzling. At one time nobody seemed to know where eels came from. Aristotle remarked, 'I have investigated the matter. In muddy pools that have been drained, eels will make their appearance once more after a fall of rain. This fact has led me to think that eels come from what are called the "bowels of the earth".' He also pointed out that eels migrate to the sea. Pliny the Elder wrote, 'In order to reproduce its kind the eel rubs itself on rocks. Pieces of its skin become detached and form young eels.' Ideas were just as confused in the sixteenth century: 'If into a muddy and shallow pool we throw some hairs from a stallion's mane then eels will be born of them'. Not until 1920 did scientists discover that eels are born far out in the Atlantic Ocean in the weed-covered Sargasso Sea. But how do the tiny eels find their way to the rivers of Britain and Europe? No one knows for

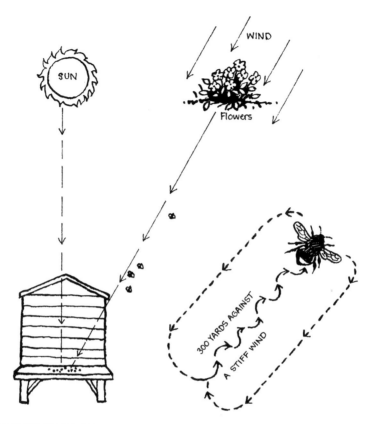

Bees' directional dances.

certain, but experiments have proved that eels can feel a
difference in temperature of anything between $3/100°$ and
$1/10°$ C. They live and move and feed keeping within
the stream of water at the correct temperature. Once they
reach the rivers they form a huge 'rope', all entwining
together, pulling themselves and each other past obstacles.
When fully mature, after ten or more years, they return to
the Sargasso Sea, where each female will lay up to 10 million
eggs before she dies.

Bees, though they usually only navigate over short
distances, are remarkable in that they can pass on 'flight
instructions' to other bees so that they too can locate a

177

distant source of food. Though they use landmarks to identify their home ground and the general area where food has been found before, they too make use of the sun's position in the sky if the area is quite featureless.

When a bee returns to the hive having discovered a new source of nectar, it will perform one of two 'dances' on the inside walls of the hive or on the 'landing strip' outside the hive. The simplest dance is the 'round dance' which merely tells the other bees that a new supply of nectar will be found within 100 metres of the hive. The second dance is the 'figure-of-eight dance', which indicates that food will be found further than 100 metres from the hive. However, the manner in which this dance is performed, its angle to the vertical and the number of waggles that the bee gives with its abdomen tells the other bees the direction and distance of the new supply. If the supply is between the hive and the sun, the centre line of the dance will be performed straight *up* the wall of the hive. If the bees have to fly away from the sun, then he dances *down* the wall; and if the food is at an angle to the sun, then the centre line of the dance will make that same angle with the vertical. As this central portion of the dance is performed, the bee waggles its abdomen from side to side. The number of waggles says how much effort had to be made to reach the food. A flight of two hundred yards against the wind would receive the same number of waggles as one of four hundred yards with the wind. Height is the one dimension that defeats the bees. Experimenters hauled food to the top of a high radio tower. On their return, the bees' dances showed no set pattern at all, for their 'language' failed them.

It may seem a long way from bee dances to Pioneer 10, launched on February 28th 1972 towards Jupiter. On board is a small metal plaque that carries Humanity's Bee Dance. The figures and lines will perhaps tell some far distant intelligence something about earth. Two naked figures indicate our shape; behind them are the plans of Pioneer 10, drawn to the same scale so that our size may be gauged. Fourteen

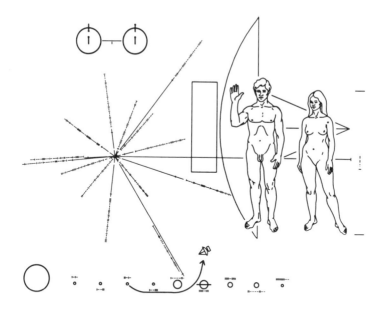

Design on the plaque of Pioneer 10. Courtesy of the National Aeronautics and Space Administration, Washington, D.C., U.S.A.

lines forming a star-like pattern represent the 14 Pulsars (sources of pulsating radio energy) in the Milky Way. Once these have been identified then the sun of our own solar system can be pin-pointed. The small circles represent the sun and the planets, with the path of Pioneer 10 passing between Jupiter and Saturn some time after December 1973. For a further seven or eight years scientists hope to receive radio signals as Pioneer 10 heads for the boundaries of our solar system. Beyond that there are no boundaries to eternity.

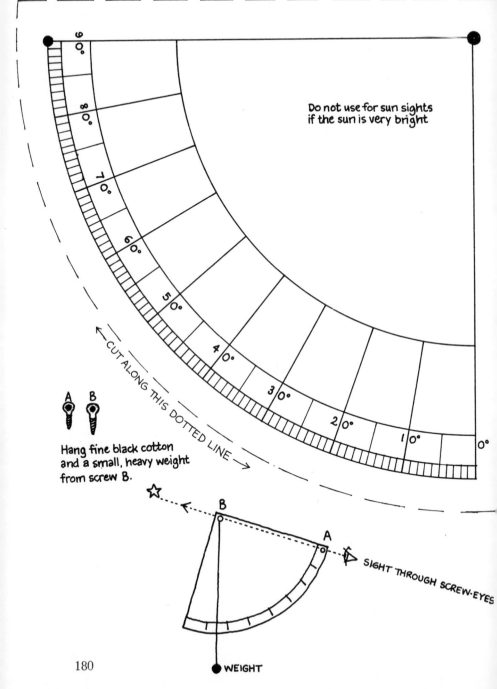

A – very small screw-eye

B – small screw

← CUT ALONG THIS DOTTED LINE →

90°

80°

70°

60°

50°

40°

30°

20°

10°

0°

Do not use for sun sights if the sun is very bright

← CUT ALONG THIS DOTTED LINE →

A   B

Hang fine black cotton and a small, heavy weight from screw B.

B

A

SIGHT THROUGH SCREW-EYES

WEIGHT

180

APPENDIX A

Making a quadrant

1 Trace or copy the drawing and cut round the broken line.

2 Stick your tracing on to a piece of plywood cut to shape.

3 Screw in the small screw eyes at A and B. (Make sure these are accurately positioned where the lines meet.)

4 Hang a small heavy weight from screw-eye B. Use black cotton.

5 If you wish your quadrant to last, give it a light coat of paper varnish.

Making an astrolabe

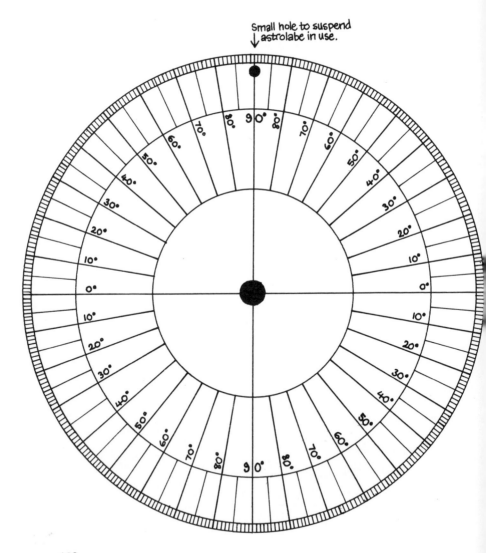

Small hole to suspend
↓ astrolabe in use.

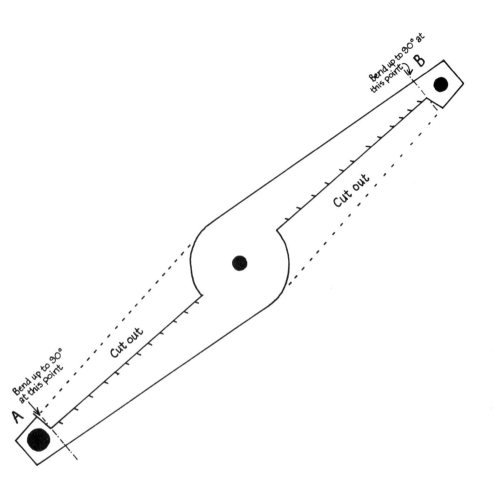

1 Carefully trace the drawing, cut out the circle and glue it on to a piece of plywood cut to size.

2 Trace the pointer on to thin tin or cardboard. Cut out this shape. The marked edges *must* be straight and *must* pass through the centre point. Drill an 8 mm (or ¼ in.) hole at A, and a 4 mm (or ⅛ in.) hole at B.

3 Bend up the sighting vanes at 90°.

4 Drill 4 mm holes in the centres of the astrolabe and pointer.

5 Mount the pointer, using a tight-fitting bolt and a thin brass washer or Perspex cut to size between the two parts.

6 Drill a small hole in the rim of the astrolabe and suspend it from a loop of cord.

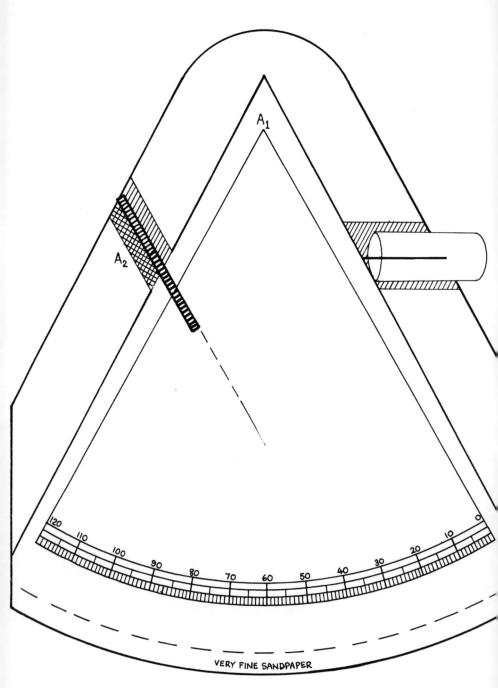

A_1

A_2

120 110 100 90 80 70 60 50 40 30 20 10 0

VERY FINE SANDPAPER

APPENDIX C

Making a sextant

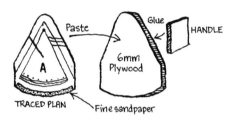

1 Trace the printed outline and paste carefully on to a prepared piece of 6 mm plywood. Coat the tracing with a thin layer of varnish. Drill a 4 mm hole exactly at point A_1. Glue a 10 cm x 5 cm x 6 mm block to the back of the sextant as a handle. Cut a 6 mm wide curve of very fine sandpaper and glue it along the lower, curved edge of the sextant.

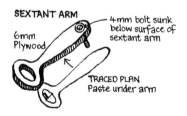

2 Trace the outline of the sextant arm (page 186). To ensure full 60° movement, it is important to shape the arm as shown. Drill out the large viewing hole and smooth the edges with a rasp. Paste the traced plan on to the underside of the arm. Drill a 4 mm hole exactly through point B_1. Sink the head of a 4 mm dia. bolt below the level of the surface of the arm. Varnish lightly all over. Stick a small section of very fine sandpaper on the underside of the arm, so that it bears against the sandpaper on the body of the sextant. This will provide friction so that the arm will not slip once a reading has been taken.

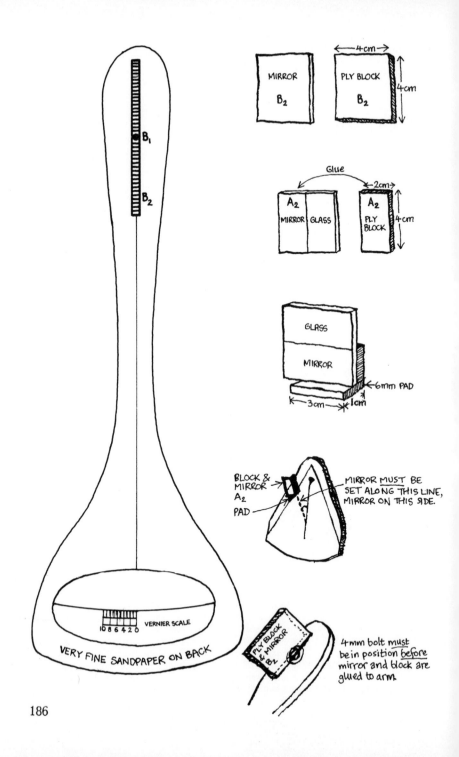

MIRROR
B₂

←4cm→
PLY BLOCK
B₂
4cm

Glue

A₂
MIRROR GLASS

←2cm→
A₂
PLY
BLOCK
4cm

GLASS

MIRROR

←6mm PAD
←3cm→ ←1cm→

BLOCK &
MIRROR
A₂
PAD

MIRROR MUST BE
SET ALONG THIS LINE,
MIRROR ON THIS SIDE.

B₁

B₂

10 8 6 4 2 0   VERNIER SCALE

VERY FINE SANDPAPER ON BACK

PLY BLOCK
& MIRROR
B₂

4mm bolt must
be in position before
mirror and block are
glued to arm.

186

3 Have a small hand mirror cut into two 4 cm squares. From the back of one mirror only scrape half of the silvering. Leave the other half fully silvered. Have two small blocks accurately cut and planed so that all angles are 90° and finished to these sizes: Block A_2 – 4 cm x 2 cm x 6 mm; Block B_2 – 4 cm x 4 cm x 6 mm. Stick the fully silvered mirror to block B_2. Stick the half silvered mirror to block A_2, so that the block is stuck against the back of the mirror half. Use the thinnest possible smear of Araldite glue. Mirror and block A_2 will then have to be mounted onto a further 6 mm pad of plywood to bring them level with B_2 mounted on the sextant arm.

4 The A_2 mirror must be glued to the body of the sextant exactly along the line marked on the plan. The pad should not extend inwards beyond the inner heavy line.

5 Mirror B_2 and its small back block should be glued on to the sextant arm, so that the surface of the mirror is along the line marked down the centre of the arm. See that the 4 mm bolt is in position before the mirror is glued into place.

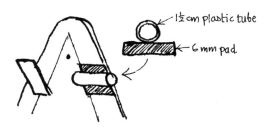
1½ cm plastic tube
6 mm pad.

6 Get a short (4 cm) length of plastic water pipe, about 1½ cm in diameter, as used by plumbers. Rub one side on sandpaper until you have a flat surface. Glue the flat surface to a 6 mm pad of plywood, and then glue this to the body of the sextant along the line marked. The pad should not extend inside the heavy line.

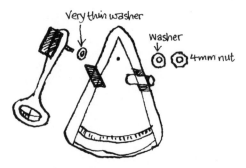

Very thin washer

Washer

4mm nut

7 Assemble the completed arm by passing the bolt, B_1, through hole A_1, with a very thin brass washer between the arm and the main body of the sextant. Tighten the nut on the other side until there is smooth movement but no looseness. When the arm is pressed against the main body, the two pieces of sandpaper should engage to make a non-slip surface.

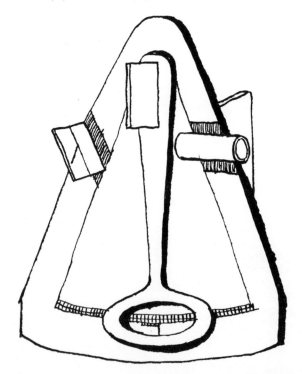

8 The completed sextant. When the instrument is being used with the sun, a layer or two of coloured paper should be folded over the end of the sighting tube and held with an elastic band. **Do not stare at the sun for long.**

APPENDIX D

Stars in the northern sky

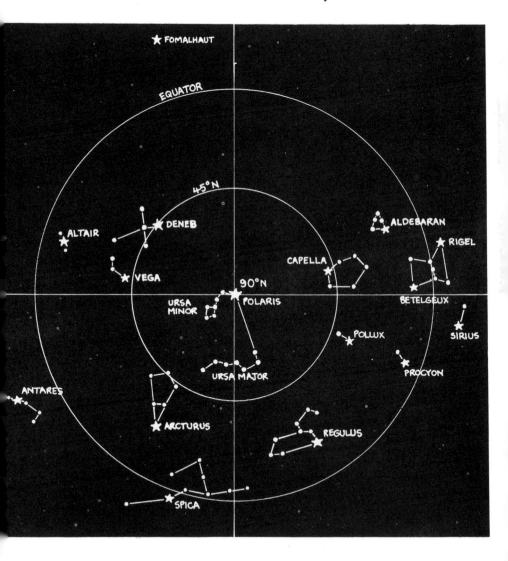

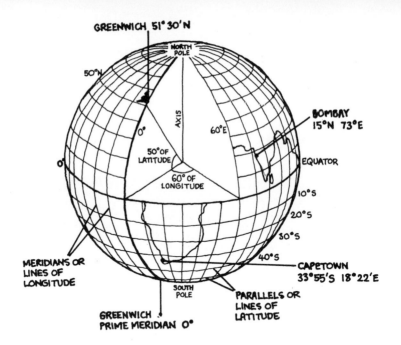

GREENWICH 51° 30' N
NORTH POLE
50°N
AXIS
BOMBAY 15°N 73°E
0°
60°E
50° OF LATITUDE
EQUATOR
0°
60° OF LONGITUDE
10°S
20°S
30°S
40°S
MERIDIANS OR LINES OF LONGITUDE
CAPETOWN 33°55'S 18°22'E
SOUTH POLE
PARALLELS OR LINES OF LATITUDE
GREENWICH PRIME MERIDIAN 0°

APPENDIX E

Latitude and Longitude

Latitude and longitude are both measurements taken from the centre of the earth (C).

Latitude is measured North and South from the Equator (0°) to the poles (90°), and the figure is always followed by N. or S. to show in which hemisphere the position is. Lines of latitude are always parallel.

Longitude is measured East and West from the Greenwich or Prime Meridian to the 180° meridian. The International Date Line follows the 180° meridian, except where this passes over land.

The length of 1° of latitude or longitude varies. Because the earth is not a true sphere, 1° of latitude

at the Equator = 68·704 st. ml (110·565 km)
at 45° N. or S. = 69·054 st. ml (111·128 km)
at 88° N. or S. = 69·407 st. ml (111·696 km)

The length of 1° of longitude shrinks from its greatest length. 1° of longitude

at the Equator = 69·172 st. ml (111·318 km)
at 45° N. or S. = 48·995 st. ml (78·847 km)
at 70° N. or S. = 23·729 st. ml (38·187 km)
at the poles = 0

190

A short bibliography

General History of Navigation
Cary, M., and Warmington, E. H., *The Ancient Explorers*, 1929.
Gatty, H., *The Raft Book*, 1943.
Hewson, J. B., *A History of the Practice of Navigation*, Brown, 1951.
Taylor, E. G. R., *The Haven Finding Art*, Hollis & Carter, 1971.
Penrose, Boise, *Travel and Discovery in the Renaissance*, Harvard U.P., 1963.
Waters, D. W., *The Art of Navigation in England in the Elizabethan and Early Stuart Times*, 1958.

Polynesian Navigation
Hilder, Brett, *Polynesian Navigation*, 1963.
Lewis, David, *We Navigators*, 1972.
Sharp, Andrew, *Ancient Voyagers in the Pacific*, 1956.

Norse Navigation
Gathorne-Hardy, R., *Norse Discoverers of America*, Oxford University Press, 1921.
Ingstad, H., *Westward to Vinland*, Jonathan Cape, 1969.
Jones, Gwyn, *The Norse Atlantic Saga*, 1964.

Some Famous Navigators
Landström, Björn, *Columbus*, Allen & Unwin, 1967.
Williamson, James A. (Ed.), *The Cabot Voyages and Bristol Discovery Under Henry VII*, Cambridge University Press, 1962.
Drake, Sir Francis, *The World Encompassed*, Ed. W. Vaux, 1854.
Cook, Capt. James, *Journals*, Ed. J. C. Beaglehole, Cambridge University Press, 1955–1967.
Guillmard, S. H., *Life of Ferdinand Magellan*.
Stanley, Hon. E. E., *The Three Voyages of Vasco da Gama*, 1869.

Navigation Today
Anderson, E. W., *Principles of Navigation*, Hollis & Carter, 1966.
Anderson, E. W., *Principles of Air Navigation*, 1951.
Admiralty Manual of Navigation, 1954.
Bowditch, *American Practical Navigator*, 1958.
Weems, P. V. H., *Air Navigation*, 1955.

Index

Altimeter, 117
Andrea Doria, 167–170
Asdic, 98, 100
Association, 76
Astrolabe, 53–54, 182–183

Back staff, 52
Balloon, 114
Bees, 177–178
Birds, 22, 27, 28, 173–176
Birkenhead, 86
Bleu, 125–126
Buoy, 142–149

Cabot, John and Sebastian, 54–57
Canoe, 28–29
Carta Pisana, 34–35
Chancellor, Richard, 57
Chart, 23–24, 34–35, 67, 151
Chichester, Francis, 115–120
Chronometer, 77–79
Clock, 69, 77–79
Columbus, Christopher, 41–45, 56, 58
Compass, 31–33, 35–38, 48, 106–107, 122–123, 145
Computer, 112–113, 126
Cook, Captain, 78–82, 84
Coracle, 11–12
Cross staff, 52
Curragh, 11–12

Darius of Persia, 7–8, 10–12
Decca, 103–104
Dectra, 103, 105
Doppler effect, 98–101, 113
Drake, Francis, 64–68
Drift, 118–121

Echo sounder, 98–100
Eels, 174, 176–177
Eirik the Red, 20
Eiriksson, Leif, 21
Elingamite, 166–167

Fixing position, 154–160
Flamsteed, John, 72
Flat earth, 12–13
Floki, 18
Fresnel lens, 135, 137

Garda, 17–18
George, 125
Globe, 40, 55
Golden Hind, 65–67
Gyro compass, 106–107

Halley, Edmond, 84
Harrison, John, 77–79
Henry the Navigator, 41
Kamal, 51

Latitude, 38, 51, 190
Laying off a course, 152–154
Lighthouse, 131–141
Lightship, 138–139, 140
Log, 46, 50, 85–88
Longitude, 38, 50–51, 69, 71, 84, 190
Loran, 105–106

Magellan, Ferdinand, 58–64
Map projection, 38–40, 151
Matthew, 54
Mayflower, 139
Mercator, 38, 151
Migration, 173–176

Nautilus, 107–112
Newton, Isaac, 73, 75, 82
Nocturnal, 71

Octant, 88–89

Pharos, 9, 132–133
Pioneer, 10, 179
Pole Star, 46–47, 71
Prime Meridian, 83–84
Ptolemy, 8

Quadrant, 180–181

Radar, 101–102, 167–170
RDF, 103
Resolution, 78–82
Royal Observatory, 72–73

Sacred calabash, 24
St. Brendan, 16–17
Sans, 112–113
San Antonio, 58–62
Santa Maria, 44–45, 48
Satellite, 112–113, 126–130
Sextant, 88, 89–93, 124–125, 184–188
Stockholm, 167–170
Submarine, 106–112
Suez Canal, 10–12
Sumner, Captain, 94–96

Telescope, 72–75
Tide, 16, 144, 160–165
Torrey Canyon, 171–172
Traverse board, 49–50
Trinidad, 58–64

Vespucci, Amerigo, 56, 58

Waves, 14